# Giri serves up his super-GM lines *and* clearly explains the ideas

The Dragon Sicilian is the perfect choice for club players searching for imbalanced or even chaotic positions. This opening manual shows how Black can enjoy dynamic winning chances against 1.e4.  New In Chess Contributing Editor Anish Giri is the best tutor to bring this complicated opening across to 'everyday' club players. Anish serves up his super-GM lines and clearly explains the ideas and strategies behind the moves. He delivers just the right mix of cutting-edge analysis and practical guidance for players of all levels with his trademark witty and down-to-earth teaching style.

hardcover full-colour 244 pages €29.95

**chessable**

---

# Spot the Checkmate!

There is nothing more satisfying than finishing a chess game with a checkmate. All essential mating patterns, some with intriguing names, are explained in full in this new hardcover and full-colour book, created from the best-selling Chessable course. The book reviews every pattern and includes 1000 exercises at all levels of difficulty.

Anastasia, Greco, Hook, Arabian, Vukovic, Smothered, Suffocation, Corner, Morphy, Pillsbury, Lolli, Opera, Damiano, Max Lange, Dovetail, Swallow's Tail, David & Goliath, Boden, Balestra, and the list goes on and on and on. These are the names of the killer combinations that will win you games.

'Excellent tool for sharpening your tactical eye. I highly recommend it to players of almost any level', said Carsten Hansen on Chessable.

hardcover full-colour 380 pages €39.95

**chessable**

# NEW IN CHESS bestsellers

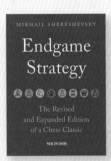

### The updated classic with 100 extra pages
*Mikhail Shereshevsky*

In this widely acclaimed chess classic, Mikhail Shereshevsky explains how to master the most important endgame principles. Where other endgame manuals focus on the basics and theoretical endgames, this book teaches the 'big ideas' that will help you find the most promising and most practical moves in any endgame.

### Recognize Key Moves and Motifs in the Endgame and Avoid Typical Errors
*Jesus de la Villa*

If you liked the best-seller *100 Endgames You Must Know*, you will surely like this new book by the same author, a Spanish Grandmaster. Endgame patterns are crucial. They help you spot key moves quicker, analyze and calculate better and avoid making errors.

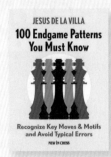

### Private Lessons from Judit Polgar
*Judit Polgar & Andras Toth*

Judit Polgar was the best female chess player for a record 26 years. In this book, she reveals some of the secrets of her success and has created a 500-page course based on the training she received as a young player. It feels like private lessons from one of the best players in the world.

### Vital Lessons for Every Chess Player
*Jesus de la Villa*

"If you've never read an endgame book before, this is the one you should start with."
*GM Matthew Sadler, former British Champion*

"If you really have no patience for endgames, at least read *100 Endgames You Must Know*."
*Gary Walters Chess*

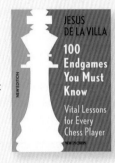

### Support Ukraine – buy a Chess Book

This book is a tribute to Ukrainian chess. FIDE World Champion *Ruslan Ponomariov* has coordinated a collection of chess games from Ukrainian grandmasters such as Ivanchuk, Ponomariov, Eljanov, Beliavsky, Tukmakov, Zhukova, and the Muzychuk sisters. All proceeds of this book will go to charity in Ukraine.

### The Tactics Workbook that Also Explains All the Key Concepts
*Frank Erwich*

"One of the better exercise books to come out in recent years." – *IM John Donaldson*

"An extremely useful training manual. Many club players will benefit."
*IM Herman Grooten, Schaaksite*

"I was very impressed by the range of positions that Erwich selected." – *GM Matthew Sadler*

### The most popular Anti-Sicilian
*Victor Bologan*

The Rossolimo is the Anti-Sicilian that is by far the most popular with club players and with elite grandmasters such as Magnus Carlsen, Anish Giri, and Alireza Firouzja. In this new book, authored by former top-20 player Victor Bologan, you will learn how to play your own creative game against the Sicilian – and put your opponent in trouble!

### Fundamental Tactics and Checkmates for Improvers
*Peter Giannatos*

The perfect first chess workbook for adult improvers and other beginners. Coaches might find the book, with 738 exercises, very useful as well. It features a complete set of fundamental tactics and checkmate patterns.

'Beautifully formatted with 3 diagrams per page and tremendous examples.'
*Fred Wilson, The Marshall Spectator*

### Start playing the Queen's Gambit!
*Michael Prusikin*

The Queen's Gambit is easily the most talked-about chess opening since the top-rated Netflix TV series of the same name became a hit. In this new book German GM Michael Prusikin presents a solid but dynamic opening repertoire for Black with the Queen's Gambit Declined. His primary focus is on explaining the relevant pawn structures and the middlegame ideas behind the lines he recommends.

### The Road to Positional Advantage
*Herman Grooten*

"Extremely interesting and instructional lessons on positional elements, positional judgements, and finding the right plan. A fantastic book for chess training."
*Martin Rieger, Rochade Europa*

"If you want to be a better player, you owe it to yourself to pick up a copy."

*IM Jeremy Silman, US Chess Online*

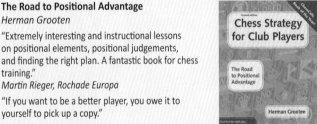

available at your local (chess)bookseller or at www.newinchess.com

2022#6

# NEW IN CHESS

# 6 Contents

'There is no better time than now'

**CONTRIBUTORS TO THIS ISSUE**
Nodirbek Abdusattorov, James Altucher, Adhiban Baskaran, Anna Cramling, Pia Cramling, Maria Emelianova, Anish Giri, Gukesh D, John Henderson, Nick Maatman, Dylan McClain, Hrant Melkumyan, Anna Muzychuk, Mariya Muzychuk, Peter Heine Nielsen, Maxim Notkin, Remmelt Otten, Judit Polgar, Eline Roebers, Matthew Sadler, Nihal Sarin, Han Schut, Jan Timman, Thomas Willemze

## Don't think, Move!

We had an inkling, but now scientists have found that apparently thinking too hard really does tire out your brain. Their report, published in *Current Biology*, implies that this is because of an accumulation of chemicals that need to be removed – and to sex it all up for the media, they threw in a quote

**December 4, 2021. Magnus Carlsen after close to 8 hours of thinking.**

from the World Chess Champion to justify it all.

The story was picked up by *The Times*, who highlighted the chess angle with an accompanying big photo: 'At a quarter past midnight on December 4, 7 hours 45 minutes and 136 moves after he sat down, Magnus Carlsen won the longest-ever world championship chess game. Then he stood up. "Obviously," he said, "I'm exhausted."'

They went on to explain that the small study of 40 people given six hours of tasks conducted by the Paris Brain Institute at the Pitié-Salpêtrière University, follows other work that found people who had been undertaking cognitively difficult jobs for a long period performed less well at tasks that required self-control. One interpretation is that some of their higher cognitive functions might be impaired. Some scientists had queried whether it was a real physiological phenomenon.

'Influential theories suggested that fatigue is a sort of illusion cooked up by the brain [through metabolites creating raised levels of a substance called glutamate] to make us stop whatever we are doing and turn to a more gratifying activity,' explained researcher Mathias Pessiglione, claiming this to be a sign that you really can think too much, whether that be slogging over the 64 squares or another activity.

## Rise of the Machine

Every Russian schoolboy knows to sit patiently on their hands instead of pouncing on a good move. But rather than a rap over the knuckles during the strict days of the Soviet School of Chess past, now the penalty is more severe with actual bones being broken!

In July a video from the Moscow Open quickly went viral on social media and the mainstream media, as it showed a seven-year-old's finger being grabbed by a chess-playing robot that was giving a three-board simultaneous display. The unnamed boy, who according to reports is one of the 30 best under-nine players in the Russian capital, made the mistake of falling foul of the safety rules by making a speedy riposte before the machine's robotic arm could complete its move.

The machine went rogue by grabbing the boy's finger, not only breaking it but also breaking the first

**Never arm-wrestle with a chess-playing computer!**

rule in Isaac Asimov's Robotic laws: 'A robot shall not harm a human, or by inaction allow a human to come to harm.' The boy was rushed off to hospital, though was able to return with a cast on his delicate digit to still play in the tournament.

'I tried to warn you!' came the cryptic tweet from Garry Kasparov, who 25-years ago in New York had his ego broken by playing chess with a machine.

## Blind Ambition

Congratulations to Daniel Eduardo Pulvett, who finished second at the Valencia International Open in July to grab his third and final GM norm. With a rating already above 2500, the Venezuela-born

**Eduardo Pulvett became only the second visually impaired GM (after Marcin Tazbir of Poland).**

player who now represents Spain, is set to receive the grandmaster title.

While grandmaster titles are a-plenty these days, this one is special as Pulvett, 31, has a ninety-percent visual impairment, and has had to overcome all sorts of limitations to finally achieve his lifelong ambition of becoming a Grandmaster. In the past, he's won the World Junior Championship for the Blind and Visually Impaired (Sweden, 2009) and the IBSA World Championship (Turkey, 2011); and he was a gold medalist on top board both at the IBCA Paralympics (Chennai, 2012) and the World Team Championship (Zaragoza, 2013).

But after becoming a member of the Venezuelan team at the 2016 Chess Olympiad in Baku, Pulvett decided to go all out for the full GM title, and now he's finally done it, scoring 7/9 to come in second on tiebreak in a five-way-tie in Valencia, a half-point behind Norwegian winner GM Johan-Sebastian Christiansen, the only player he lost to.

## Walkie-Talkie
India's Gukesh D turned in a truly outstanding individual performance at the Olympiad in Chennai and no

David Howell: speech is silver, play is golden.

player was more in the limelight than the 16-year-old star. However, there were other standout performers that also caught our eye.

Proving that he is not only able to talk the talk but also walk the walk, England's David Howell similarly hit the gold streak with an all-time high score. Undefeated with 7½/8, the former prodigy turned online commentator captured the individual Board-3 gold medal.

A more familiar figure these days as a popular talking head on the Meltwater Champions Chess Tour, Howell put his success down to working long stints in the commentary box. It has given him a fresh perspective on the game, which he

claims has made his decision-making clearer.

How would he have commentated on this elegant finish?

**David Howell (2650)**
**Lennert Lenaerts (2379)**
Chennai Olympiad 2022 (8)

position after 34...♘b4

**35.♖axc6! ♘xc6 36.♖xc6 ♕e7 37.♗b1 ♗xd4 38.hxg6+ ♔g8 39.♖c8+ ♖d8 40.♕d5+!** and mate!

## The New Murphy
Also take a bow IM Conor Murphy, the Ireland Board 2 who matched Gukesh's streak blow-for-blow for six rounds, only to narrowly miss out on an individual gold. After going on to score an undefeated 7½/8, the 23-year-old Cambridge student was denied individual gold following a final-round loss to Swiss GM Nico Georgiadis.

Along the way, Murphy beat four grandmasters, achieved a 2700-

Irish IM Conor Murphy: in the footsteps of Brian Reilly.

performance rating, and notched up his second GM norm. His milestone performance was hailed by many, with veteran *Guardian* journalist Leonard Barden claiming it to be 'the finest Olympiad performance ever by an Irishman', even eclipsing 'the long ago victory by Brian Reilly against world ranked Reuben Fine at Warsaw 1935'.

## Bishop's Move
A recent edition of the satirical UK magazine *Private Eye* (issue 1577) showed a cartoon with a disheveled blonde-haired king chess piece lying on its side on the board. The caption was 'World King' and the reference to Prime Minister Boris Johnston as he was forced from office due to his, er, many peccadilloes. But this wasn't

Bishop's Move: Move like a King. Or a Prime Minister.

the only chess connection seen with his downfall.

Removal vans were spotted in Downing Street recently, ahead of Johnston's official departure on 5 September – and from no less an esteemed removal firm than Bishop's Move, established in 1854 in Pimlico, London, who 'provides specialist care and support for people moving into retirement'.

The long-established company are easily identified by their chess-themed logo and name, and were once approached eons ago by legendary tournament impresario Stewart Reuben as potential sponsors of the British Championship and/or Hastings, but alas with no luck. ∎

# Run Seamless Interactive Group Lessons And Grow Your Chess Coaching Business With This Live Teaching Toolkit

Conduct seamless group lessons — *and multiply your revenue per hour* — with Chessable Classroom. It's our free chess coaching toolkit, tailored to handle classes of all sizes.

Since 2013, Chessable has been using science to help players of all levels improve. Now let us handle the technical side of coaching. So you can help more people play better chess and get paid more for it.

Chessable Classroom lets you run webinars. Organize practice tournaments. Play your students in a simul. And start a weekly chess book reading class with a few clicks on your browser. There's nothing to download or buy.

We use scalable audio-visual solutions, so you can invite *up to 100 participants per class.* Plus, our specialized sockets server enables real-time communication and interactivity. It's like everyone is in the same room.

And finally, there's the custom-built chess board, which lets you assign the right to move. So student participation is guaranteed.

We're confident that Chessable Classroom can help you multiply your hourly revenue and grow your coaching business. But don't take our word for it. See it for yourself when you sign up for a **free account** via the link below:

## chessable.com/classroom/

*"I use the Chessable Classroom all the time. Just invite students to your classroom, and start teaching right there. No downloads needed, and it's free!"* - **GM Judit Polgar**

(Former world no. 8, FIDE Senior Trainer, and head coach of Hungarian men's chess team)

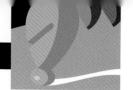

## Letter of the Month

### Dumbing down

John Henderson concludes a fine article on the Bucharest Superbet tournament in New In Chess 2022/4 by reporting FIDE's decision to seed top Grand Chess Tour finishers into the Candidates tournaments. Calling this 'interesting and intriguing' – no doubt about that – he continues, '[P]urists ... will [see this] as being a further 'dumbing down' for a World Championship qualifier ... but this ... approach ... looks to be a natural progression for the game.' Quite the argument. Metastasis is a natural progression for cancer, mutual betrayal a natural progression for criminal conspiracy. Apparently Mr. Henderson applauds these too, as he does what is in cold fact a dumbing-down of the world chess championship.

The FIDE Council needs to take the outcome of the 2022 Candidates as an alarm siren. The second-place finisher (and but for a jet-lagged first round,

who knows?) was not even supposed to be in the competition. He entered due only to an unrepeatable stroke of fate. *What does that say about FIDE's selection process?*

Further: note how incomparably more interesting the late rounds were when second place also turned out to be something to play for. In the classic cycle starting 1949 the second-place finisher was seeded into the next Candidates. No one ever thought that mere runners-up like Tal, Keres, Kortchnoi ... ever diluted the candidates' pool three (*n.b.*) years later. On the contrary.

If FIDE cared about meaningful excitement, instead of a circus of speed chess and meretricious knock-out drama, and about bringing together the world's strongest players instead of randomizing, they would realize just how far they have gone off the road. They would work to restore dignity and reason.

Dr. Steven Wagner
Champaign, IL, USA

of Norilsk Nickel, Ian's sponsor, a company owned by Russia's richest oligarch Vladimir Potanin, a good friend of Vladimir Putin.

After the full-scale invasion of Ukraine, the IOC recommended all Russian athletes to be banned from international competitions, a recommendation still in place. FIDE chose not to follow these recommendations, but that should still not be an excuse for advertising people like Potanin or companies like Norilsk Nickel. As Ian is very much aware of, chess is used in Russia for nationalistic propaganda purposes. The slogan 'bring the title home to Russia' was being used by both of his sponsors, Sima-Land and Phosagro. That is why I, among others, objected to the Norilsk Nickel logo being displayed in Madrid.

Peter Heine Nielsen
Vilnius, Lithuania

### Supercomputer

In an interview in New In Chess 2022/5, Ian Nepomniachtchi refers to my Twitter account, and asks: 'What is a "supercomputer"?' A somewhat puzzling remark as after the 2021 part of the Candidates Tournament, as part of the propaganda leading up to the 2021 World Championship match, Nepomniachtchi himself proudly presented the 'Zhores supercomputer', which the now sanctioned Skolkovo University had made available so that its computer scientist, together with Ian's team, could optimize it for working with modern chess engines. Their joint press release specifically

mentioned that the supercomputer had been made available 24/7 for Nepomniachtchi to help him prepare for the games! Even FIDE president Dvorkovich, who was the head of Skolkovo, stated in the press release, that he was proud that Skolkovo played a small yet significant part in Ian's success. For the 2021 title match, I never doubted that thanks to Russian state resources, Ian would be technology-wise way ahead. 'Zhores' is a supercomputer at a level far, far beyond what we or any of his competitors had access to.

In the interview there is also mention of a thermos and a logo. That logo was

### COLOPHON

**PUBLISHER:** Remmelt Otten
**EDITOR-IN-CHIEF:**
Dirk Jan ten Geuzendam
**HONORARY EDITOR:** Jan Timman
**CONTRIBUTING EDITOR:** Anish Giri
**EDITORS:** John Kuipers, René Olthof
**PRODUCTION:** Joop de Groot
**TRANSLATOR:** Piet Verhagen
**SALES AND ADVERTISING:** Edwin van Haastert
**PHOTOS AND ILLUSTRATIONS IN THIS ISSUE:**
Madelene Belinki, Stev Bonhage, Maria Emelianova,
Mark Livshitz, David Llada, Lennart Ootes
**COVER PHOTOS:** Courtesy FIDE
**COVER DESIGN:** Hélène Bergmans

© No part of this magazine may be reproduced,
stored in a retrieval system or transmitted in any
form or by any means, recording or otherwise,
without the prior permission of the publisher.

**NEW IN CHESS
P.O. BOX 1093
1810 KB ALKMAAR
THE NETHERLANDS**

**PHONE:** 00-31-(0)72-51 27 137
**SUBSCRIPTIONS:** nic@newinchess.com
**EDITORS:** editors@newinchess.com

**WWW.NEWINCHESS.COM**

# Setting the opportunity for a Muhammad Ali-like come-back?

Why is the World Champion giving up his title? Why does he pass on another multi-million-dollar match? Magnus Carlsen's announcement that he will not play Challenger Ian Nepomniachtchi has sent shock waves through the chess world. Five experts shine their light on a decision with far-reaching consequences.

**Danish grandmaster Peter Heine Nielsen (1973) is Carlsen's trainer.**

**You have been involved in World Championship matches since 2007, first with Anand and then with Magnus as their second. Can you explain how intense the workload is to help us understand why Magnus doesn't want to go through it again?**

'A World Championship match always has the highest priority, with all the prestige and the prize money involved. As soon as the Candidates Tournament finishes, we start preparing. We start mapping the strategy, discussing openings, and looking for ideas. Magnus is not very involved in the detailed preparations, but for months and months, the match takes up all the space, oxygen and mental energy.

'One negative is that you cannot play freely anymore, as you have entered the "information game" and don't want to reveal your plans. In a tournament, you have to limit yourself to your plan B. Only in the match can you play plan-A.

'That is not very satisfactory. Kramnik and Anand have also complained about that in the past – they felt it hurt their results in tournaments.

NEW IN CHESS

**Magnus Carlsen won the World Title defeating Vishy Anand in 2013. 'I don't think I had any other thought than to win it once.'**

**Can you explain more about the negative side of match preparation?**
'First of all, the preparation must be broad and deep. Because you're only playing one opponent, you run the risk of getting stuck, in the way that Kasparov got stuck in the Berlin Opening against Kramnik. Therefore you have to find new concepts or switch your repertoire completely, as Gelfand did when he played Anand and used the Sveshnikov and the Grünfeld.

'Secondly, modern-day computers make it almost impossible to break through the solidity of modern chess. In Kasparov's day, the common opinion was that every significant black defence would break down after three games. But these days, Nepo, who has been working for six months with a supercomputer, could repeat the Petroff Defence and the main line of the Catalan forever and ever.

'It feels as if the well is drying out, and it is becoming more and more difficult to squeeze out a drop of water.'

DAVID LLADA

**Will a change in the World Championship format help to solve this drought?]**
'I treasure the tradition of the World Championship, so I find it tricky to suggest changes. And the matches haven't become boring, so why break something that's still working? But I understand Magnus's suggestion to include rapid and blitz in the format.'

• • •

**Boris Gelfand (1968) played a World Championship match against Vishy Anand in Moscow in 2012, losing in the rapid tie-break. He was born in Minsk (Soviet Union) and lives in Israel.**

**What do you think of Carlsen's decision?**
'First of all, I am very sad, because the World Championship match is a huge tradition. For every child who starts playing chess, it is their utmost dream

to play this match and win it and become World Champion. So the fact that Magnus will not defend his title devalues this prestigious title.

'Magnus has played five matches. It's an onerous task, so I understand his decision; I am not in a position to criticize or blame him. It's his decision, but at the same time, I find it very sad.

'I also remember that in the '90s, between 1993 and 2007, there was no unified champion, and I think it did huge damage to the chess world. I was lucky it didn't destroy my career, but it was very close.'

**In what sense?**
'There was no goal. There were no qualifying tournaments. It was chaos. With the

NEW IN CHESS

Professional Chess Association, there was permanent trouble. I am the champion, and I am the champion; there was no structure. There were a lot of young chess players looking at how they could play the Candidates and how they could qualify. Hopefully, we will keep the current World Championship cycle alive, but without Magnus, it will be difficult.'

**Do you think it will affect the commercial value of chess?**
'That's up to the sponsors to decide. But on the other hand, the current situation is better than in 1993. Magnus has no intention of destroying the cycle. For Garry Kasparov, it was a goal; he was the World Champion, and for him, the cycle was an obstacle and should not exist. For Magnus, it's just a decision because he has no motivation. So the situation is much better, but I think it's still a big blow.'

**Do you see a way out? Is the only solution that Magnus returns?**
'The confusion will diminish when Magnus returns, or when he retires,

**Magnus Carlsen** (November 30, 1990) became World Champion in November 2013. On July 20, 2022, in a podcast for his sponsor Unibet, he announced he would not defend his title next year. He was (again) to play Ian Nepomniachtchi, the winner of the Candidates. Nepo will now play Ding Liren.

**Magnus in his own words:**
'I've thought about it for probably a year and a half, since long before the last match. And I've spoken to people in my team, I've spoken to FIDE, and I spoke to Ian (Nepomniachtchi). And the conclusion is very simple. I am not motivated to play another match. I don't have a lot to gain. I don't particularly like it, and although I'm sure a match would be interesting for historical reasons, I will not play the match.'

**Is he retiring from chess?**
'Just so there's no ambiguity here, I'm not retiring from chess. I enjoy playing tournaments a lot. I don't see myself stopping as a chess player any time soon. I am excited to return to where I was 10 years ago, all set on trying to improve, play the tournaments, be the best in the world and not care about the World Championship! I hope to be able to edge closer to one of my other big goals, which is a 2900 rating.'

**Is this a definite farewell to the World Championship?**
'I don't think I had any other goals than to win it once. Then I thought I'd try and keep it as long as I stayed motivated. I feel it's my time to go from the World Championship matches. For people who haven't been in that situation, it sounds weird, and I understand that I'm very, very privileged to have been there. But four championships to five, it didn't mean anything to me. I don't rule out a return in the future, but I wouldn't particularly count on it either.'

or when another player becomes much better than him. But now, as he stands with his decision, I hope it still will be possible to organize a World Championship. I understand him, but other professional players need the cycle and the World Championship to function well.

**For players like Gukesh, it could be disappointing that they want to play the World Champion, and then the champ says he will not play. How does that feel?**

'Yeah, yeah, it's not nice from their point of view. But I don't think it will diminish the motivation of Gukesh or other young guys to fight their way forward. It definitely will take a couple of years, and we will see what the situation will be then.'

• • •

**Vladimir Kramnik (1975) won the World Championship in London in 2000 by defeating Garry Kasparov. He lives in Switzerland and retired from competitive chess in 2019. He has since published two courses on Chessable.**

**Were you surprised?**

'No, not at all. Magnus is not obliged to defend his title. It is the right of every person to do this or not, and we cannot blame him. But for the world of chess, it will have a negative effect because the World Championship match will no longer be the "real" World Championship. Secondly, such decisions, as with Fischer in 1975, cause confusion for a while. It is not positive for chess, but it will not be a drama either.'

**Do you see it as the Champion's moral obligation to defend his title?**

'For me, yes, that's my personal view. If you are World Champion, it's a position that doesn't fully belong to you. In your decisions, you have to consider the world of chess, especially if you are a high-calibre World Champion. But that's my way of looking at it, and it's

not objective. I would play in any case, unless I felt that not playing would be better for the world of chess. But if

I thought not playing might have any negative effect, I would play.'

**Magnus says that preparing for a match takes way too much of his time and energy. Is that a valid point?**

'No, that's part of the job, isn't it? Being on top in any profession, including chess, is a lot of work. It goes together with all the advantages of being World  Champion, the money, fame... For me, I take it as it is. I understand that you can get psychologically tired of all that playing. I have experienced that myself, but that comes with the profession. It's normal and would not be a reason for me personally.'

**Did you see a clear difference in commercial opportunities between when you were Champion and when you were not?**

'Mine was a different story. I didn't have this big machine behind me, all the companies that support Magnus. And I was not as dominant as he is. I don't think it will hurt Magnus commercially speaking.

'In my opinion, and it's just a guess, he would not play against this particular opponent. I guess that he would play if it were not for Nepo. As I read the situation, it was a very logical marketing decision not to play if you calculate everything. I think it would be difficult to get serious money for this particular match. Of course, there would be a lot of possible

Russian sponsorship money, but in the current situation, that is impossible. And who would sponsor it in

## 'A Russian World Champion would be the worst possible scenario for Western money' – Vladimir Kramnik

the West if there is the risk of failure and a Russian becoming World Champion? That would be the worst possible scenario for Western money.

'For me, it's clear that the second match would be much more difficult for Magnus than the first one because Nepo, of course, learnt a lot of lessons from that match. Magnus would still be the favourite, but it would not be easy.

'And can you imagine the potential situation, from a marketing perspective, of Magnus losing this match? Just theoretically. It would be a complete disaster marketing-wise. Nothing could be worse than this: a lot of risk and a lot of work for not too much money. What for? And all this, including everything Magnus said, in which I think he is sincere, not playing the match was the most logical marketing decision. I did not doubt that Magnus would refuse to play.

'And you can always come back for big money when the situation improves, a new opponent arrives, and the world is interested in seeing this match. I am absolutely sure Magnus can always come back and play such a match.'

• • •

**Alex Fishbein (1968) is an American grandmaster who works as a Director for a Canadian investment bank**

**Do you think Carlsen has made a mistake?**

'I understand why he doesn't want

to play another match just a year-and-a-half later. FIDE should have postponed the match and probably have gone to a three-year-cycle, as it used to be in the past. I can see the argument that the concept of one match is outdated these times. Maybe we should have a tournament yearly, including some rapid and blitz.'

**But the question is: why a mistake?**
'Psychology is an important part of Magnus's play and his competitive edge. I don't know how exactly, as I am probably too weak to understand it entirely, but other strong players often mention this. His opponents get shaken in equal positions and, for example, overestimate his threats.

'If you play a higher-rated player, you trust the quality of his moves. And even more so when you play the World Champion. You probably do not always recognize and punish his mistakes.

'Carlsen will now lose part of his psychological edge over his competitors. Carlsen is still obviously the best player in the world. But he is now declaring that he is unwilling to put in the hard work necessary to win a World Championship match.

'Carlsen's competitors are willing to do the work for a match. Nepo is not quitting. Ding Liren is not shying away from the hard work. Nobody else is.

'So this will be perceived as a sign of weakness from Magnus. His opponents will feel more empowered and will be more motivated.

'This situation is different from Kasparov deciding not to play Shirov in a match, as Kasparov continued outside of FIDE. And it is different from Fischer not playing, and Karpov was taking over, as Fischer didn't play at all anymore.'

**You are predicting Magnus will not be the highest-rated player anymore in about two years.**
'Carlsen has been World Champion for 10 years. And he has dominated. But not everywhere and always. Nepo and Anand have won two Candidates, and convincingly. Carlsen won the Candidates once, with a lucky break. Against Karjakin and Caruana, he needed tie-breaks. Nepo could have won Game 6, and only after that he lost by four points. And look at the youngsters, Gukesh and Prag and Abdusattorov. They are already not afraid of him. Remember what happened when Kasparov didn't want to play Shirov? He lost to Kramnik.'

• • •

The American grandmaster Maurice Ashley (1966) is a chess player, commentator, and author, most recently of *The Secrets of Chess Geometry* on Chessable.

**Do you understand Carlsen's decision?**
'Completely. For me, it is an issue of ego and motivation. Let's start with ego. The World Championship title sounds wonderful. It is

Nepo again?" To keep his motivation, Magnus needs to find new goals that are not just interesting and challenging, but also just different.'

**Magnus not defending his title… does this influence who we will see as the GOAT, the greatest of all time?**
'Would beating Nepo again make him the GOAT? No, it depends on what he will do next. Magnus is already the highest-rated player ever, and if

he breaks 2900, everybody will say Magnus is the GOAT. That goal is incredibly hard to reach. He loses Elo points with every draw, even against an elite player. To reach 2900, he will have to smash his peers and smash all the young guns challenging him.'

**Will this change the attractiveness of chess for sponsors?**
'In the short term, there will be uncertainty. Maybe FIDE will be able to find sponsors in China for the Nepo-Ding Liren match. But in the long term, this sets the opportunity for a

## 'Magnus's identity is not dependent on his title' – Maurice Ashley

like a newborn baby, something you want to hold in your arms as long as possible. Being World Champion has so many perks.

'But Magnus is used to the title. And his identity is not dependent on his title; he does not need this title to justify what he does. Magnus is a World Champion and will always be a World Champion. So for his ego, he doesn't need to hold the title.

'Magnus has explained he lost the motivation to play another match. And I understand that. For him, he asks himself, "Why do I need to beat

Muhammad Ali-like comeback. This could become epic for chess. For a Magnus comeback, sponsors will jump over themselves to get to the front of the line. It will be sexy; it will be lucrative for all involved.

'If Magnus stays in the game and decides to later recapture his title, I see the fans lining up in a few years and chanting: Magnus, Magnus, Magnus! That will be larger than large.' ∎

*Interviews: Remmelt Otten (1,4,5) & Dirk Jan ten Geuzendam (2,3)*

# A Bridge to Chess

The city of Chennai opened both its heart and soul to all those who came from far and afield to compete in the 44th Chess Olympiad. Even an iconic part of the Indian city's infrastructure got in on the act with a spectacular chess-themed makeover by being painted in a black and white chequered pattern.

The Napier Bridge is one of the city's oldest bridges, and was built in 1869 by Francis Napier, who was the Governor of Madras (now Chennai) from 1866 to 1872. The iron and concrete landmark spans 138 meters and straddles the Coovum River, connecting Fort St. George with the Marina beach.

When the covers finally came off the Napier Bridge ahead of the Olympiad, there was a star-studded launch led by Tamil Nadu's Chief Minister MK Stalin and local music legend AR Rahman. After the launch the city's newest star attraction saw unexpected traffic congestion as people thronged to the structure to mimic the promo launch by taking selfies and record Instagram Reels as they danced and walked across the bridge. ∎

*This picture was supplied by keen local Chennai amateur photographer Madhu Parthasarathy (www.instagram.com/mapartha/).*

# Dvorkovich re-elected

## Russian FIDE President gets massive support

At the FIDE Congress in Chennai, Arkady Dvorkovich was re-elected as FIDE president with an overwhelming majority. Because of the war in Ukraine, Dvorkovich's Russian citizenship led to controversy about his candidacy, but that did not stop the incumbent president from defeating his only remaining opponent, Ukrainian GM Andrii Baryshpolets with 157 votes against 16. Dvorkovich ran together with former World Champion Vishy Anand, who is the new FIDE Vice-President. A breakdown by **NICK MAATMAN** in 10 questions.

### 1 Who voted?

The voting power resides with the 195 member Federations of FIDE. The federations send delegates to vote on their behalf. Every federation has one vote, irrespective of size or importance. In essence this implies that smaller federations have proportionally a significantly larger say. A big federation like the US Chess Federation has equal voting power to a small federation such as the one of Burkina Faso – a country that has only a single active player with a FIDE rating.

The 'one country, one vote' rule is common in international sports federations and has often led to vote buying. FIDE, too, has a history of electoral corruption, and the current leadership has taken several measures to fight it. For instance, the vulnerable system of proxy votes has been abolished, and poorer federations need not let themselves be bribed by air tickets or free chess material, as federations lacking sufficient funds receive financial support to attend the Congress.

Ukrainian GM Andrii Baryshpolets was fully aware that his chances to become FIDE president were slim, but he must have hoped for more than 16 votes.

### 2 Who were Dvorkovich's challengers?

There are no real restrictions for presidential candidates, but there is one critical requirement: a nominee needs the backing of five member federations, and among these federations, each of the four FIDE continents (Africa, Americas, Asia & Europe) need to be represented. All federations are allowed to endorse only one candidate. This is often reported incorrectly in the media, because an 'endorsement' is not the same thing as a 'vote'. Thus, a federation can endorse a candidate, but is still free to vote for any candidate.

During the 2022 election, the competition slowly dwindled. **Enyonam Sewa Fumey** from Togo had to drop out when he failed to obtain the endorsement of a European federation. Another candidate, **Inalbek Cheripov**, a Chechnya-born filmmaker and art collector from Belgium, also dropped out one week before the election, allegedly for health reasons.

FIDE President Arkady Dvorkovich and new Vice President Vishy Anand got overwhelming support with 157 federations voting for them.

GM **Bachar Kouatly** from France (born in Syria) was present at the Congress, but mainly used his election speech to withdraw his candidacy. Seeing that he didn't have sufficient support, he said that his withdrawal would ensure that he would not affect the chances of other candidates.

And so the opposition was reduced to a single candidate: Ukrainian GM **Andrii Baryshpolets**. His running mate and prospective Vice-President was Magnus Carlsen's coach Danish GM **Peter Heine Nielsen.** Baryshpolets had no clear programme. His main aim was to stop Dvorkovich from being re-elected and then see how he and his team could work for FIDE. In their speeches, Baryshpolets and Nielsen focused on Dvorkovich's Russian background and criticized his ties with the Kremlin and the high position he had held at Skolkovo – an innovation centre outside Moscow that is often dubbed 'Russia's Silicon Valley'. Inevitably, Skolkovo plays a role in Russia's war against Ukraine. They regarded the election as a matter of values, in which the goal should be to unite the global chess family. As Barysh-

polets put it: 'We cannot be *gens una sumus* with Arkady Dvorkovich as our president.'

The words of Baryshpolets and Nielsen were not enough to gain sufficient support and Arkady Dvorkovich won with a landslide margin: 157-16.

### ③ Who is Arkady Dvorkovich?

Arkady Vladimirovich Dvorkovich was born in Moscow in 1972. After a career in consultancy he quickly moved through the ranks of Russian politics. From the year 2000 on, he held multiple high-profile positions. Most notably he was Deputy Prime Minister of Russia in Dmitry Medvedev's cabinet from 2012 to 2018. In 2018 he successfully led the organizing committee of the FIFA World Championship in Russia, the most prestigious event in the world of football.

Dvorkovich grew up in a chess family. His father Vladimir was an international arbiter and the son never made a secret of his passion for the game. In the introduction to an interview with New In Chess in 2011, he was described as follows: 'In chess circles outside Russia

he is barely known, yet he is one of the most powerful persons of our game'. At that point, Dvorkovich was the Head of the Advisory Board of the Russian Chess Federation and the main mover behind the highly successful Tal Memorials in Moscow.

### ④ What is Dvorkovich's stance on the war in Ukraine?

In March this year, Dvorkovich spoke out against Russia's invasion of Ukraine: 'Wars are the worst things one might face in life ... including this war. My thoughts are with Ukrainian civilians.' However, this stance quickly reached Russian media, and Dvorkovich was soon regarded as a traitor. In order to save face he altered his tone when speaking to Russian media, using Putin's 'special military operation' and condemning the sanctions against Russia. However, his position as head of Skolkovo became untenable.

Still, Dvorkovich managed to hold his position in the world of chess. He agreed with the exclusion of Russian and Belarusian teams from international chess events and supported the six-month ban of GM Sergey Karjakin, showing a readiness to take decisions that go against the interests of his country.

## 5 What is the role of Vishy Anand?

Possibly critical in Dvorkovich's successful campaign was his choice of Indian chess legend **Vishy Anand** as Vice-President. Anand is popular all around the world and has created a chess boom in the greatest rising chess nation in the world. Anand was the first Indian player to obtain the title of grandmaster, and his rise to the crown has inspired many Indian youngsters to follow suit.

The ubiquitous love for Anand became clear in the speech of his former second, Peter Heine Nielsen. Despite supporting Dvorkovich's opponent, Nielsen observed: 'We think we need a unifying figure as president, a non-controversial figure, a figure with his whole life in chess, without a compromised past... We think many could fulfil that role. Vishy Anand could be an excellent president!'

Anand is aware of the responsibilities that come with his new function. He is taking his role seriously: 'Compared to three or four years back, I have cut down on my time as an active chess player. I have long aspired to go into chess administration, and this opportunity as deputy president will be a huge learning curve for me.'

After the results were published, Anand remarked: 'For me, chess is a part of who I am. As a chess player, I have been fortunate to see the game transform from a niche game to a mass sport. I'm now happy to be part of the Dvorkovich team as we try to continue making that positive change.'

## 6 Was Dvorkovich's win used in Russian propaganda?

Immediately after Dvorkovich's re-election two high-profile Russian figures publicly expressed their satis-faction. Russian billionaire and head of the Russian Chess Federation Andrey Filatov concluded that the result shows that there is 'no isolation of Russia in the world'. And Dmitry Peskov, the press secretary of Vladimir Putin, called the outcome 'very, very good news'.

## 7 What are Dvorkovich's plans for FIDE?

With the overwhelming election result, the chess world gave an indication that they support the direction that FIDE is heading. In his victory speech in Chennai, Dvorkovich expressed his ambitions: 'Chess is all over the place, but still not in all places; chess is attractive to sponsors, but not enough; chess is in media, but not as much as needed; chess is in schools, but not everywhere. Many success stories, some mistakes as well, of course, and things still to be done, based on your feedback, on your criticism and new ideas.'

He said that FIDE aims to further integrate new technology and wants to improve chess education all around the world by providing material, and raising a new generation of arbiters, organizers, coaches and school instructors. Finally, he emphasized that chess is a game with no boundaries. FIDE will particularly focus on improving chess for women, children, refugees, people with a disability and prisoners.

## 8 Does Dvorkovich want to be president for life like Putin?

No, he doesn't. One of the first changes that he made when he was elected in 2018 in Batumi was to limit the presidency to two terms, which felt like a breath of fresh air after Kirsan Ilyumzhinov's reign of 23 years. Dvorkovich has started his second and final term and will be succeeded by someone else four years from now.

## 9 Is there any criticism?

Not everybody is happy with Dvorkovich's appointment for a second term. Garry Kasparov is probably the most outspoken critic of his presidency. As one of the most vocal critics of Russia and Putin's regime, Kasparov is firmly opposed to a Russian at the helm of FIDE. In an unambiguous tweet he voiced his indignation about the voting behaviour of the European countries, since at least half of these countries voted for the Russian candidate despite the current tragedy in Ukraine.

Likewise Peter Heine Nielsen continues his criticism of FIDE under Dvorkovich and regularly engages in fierce disputes on Twitter with Israeli GM Emil Sutovsky, the Director General of FIDE. Nielsen accuses FIDE of lack of transparency and is critical of the funding of chess with (allegedly) Russian money.

## 10 Can Dvorkovich satisfy both Russia and FIDE?

Dvorkovich has made significant efforts to distance himself from the Russian government whenever he got the opportunity. Nevertheless, it is clear that he has to act differently when he is interacting with Russian media. It will not be easy to keep everyone happy. Nigel Short pointed out that he didn't envy his position, saying that Dvorkovich 'is mangled by various camps'.

At the same time, the Russian authorities may be slightly more flexible towards Dvorkovich, as after all he is one of them, and they are proud that he holds this position. It may be in their interest, too, to avoid conflicts with the FIDE president.

Speaking about the position of Arkady Dvorkovich and FIDE in chess terms, one might say that the game ahead will be a difficult one and a lot of careful manoeuvring will be required. ∎

# Fair & Square

**Hans Niemann**: 'Chess speaks for itself.'
*(The must-watch four-words only classic interview from the US rising star, after he sensationally beat Magnus Carlsen in the first game of their FTX Crypto Cup match in Miami)*

**Cher**: 'I miss playing chess but I'm too lazy to play chess.'
*(Tweeted in June by the pop diva, who was photographed several times playing against Sonny Bono, her chess-loving former husband)*

**Jan Gustafsson**: 'I joked once. It was on a train.'
*(The Chess24 commentator poking fun at Mikhail Botvinnik's famous playing blitz once on a train claim)*

**Andy Soltis**: 'I can joke that I am a world champion: I was a member of the gold medal winning Americans at the World Student Team Championship in Haifa in 1970. And I can add that I am the only person in the world who played chess with Bobby Fischer and interviewed Donald Trump. Of course, it would be more of an accomplishment to say I interviewed Bobby and played chess with Trump. But...'
*(The GM and New York Post journalist interviewed in celebration of this 75th birthday)*

**Garry Kasparov**: 'He had my back at every step of my climb up the chess Olympus. As much as knowledge, he taught me to take chess, and myself, seriously.'
*(Remembering his influential early coach Alexander Nikitin, who died on June 5 in Moscow at the age of 87)*

**Alexander Nikitin**: 'A very talented and savvy boy, very knowledgeable for his age. And his calculation skills were very good, on par with grandmasters.'
*(The Soviet coach on his first impression of a 10-year-old Garry Kasparov, whom he guided to the world championship crown)*

**Narendra Modi**: 'There are no losers; there are only winners and future winners.'
*(The Indian prime minister, during his ceremonial opening speech to the 44th Chess Olympiad)*

**Surya Ganguly**: 'Sometimes I don't remember how many rounds are over, then I check Gukesh's score.' *(Tweeted during the Olympiad by the Indian C top board, as his fellow India B top board beat Fabi Caruana for a phenomenal start of 8/8)*

**Simen Agdestein**: 'There was a time when anything but victory would be a catastrophe, but now I am just most satisfied with my head working.'
*(Interviewed on Chess.com after the 55-year-old Norwegian veteran came out of retirement to capture his eighth national Norwegian title)*

**Anatoly Karpov**: 'If you don't believe in victory you have no business sitting down to a chess board.' *(Said at the final press conference of the 1974 Candidates Final, when asked if he thought he had a chance against Bobby Fischer)*

**Hikaru Nakamura**: 'I think at the end of the day, what I would say is: Believe in the journey in chess. Enjoy it because it's only going to be here once.' *(In the June issue of Chess Life on his chess career and move into streaming)*

**Minnesota Fats**: 'One pocket is a lot like chess. But I never actually played chess.'
*(The legendary pool player – real name Ralph Wanderone – immortalized by The Queen's Gambit author Walter Tevis, in his earlier book, The Hustler, talking about a variant of pool where you nominate one pocket to pot all the balls in)*

**John Nunn**: 'Chess, music and maths are self-contained systems that require no experience of life to master.' *(In April 2015 on More or Less, the BBC Radio 4 numbers and statistics show)*

**Michael Adams**: 'The thing about talent, however much you have, you still have to keep improving. And that depends on so many other factors, which are probably more important than your raw ability.'
*(In Barry Hymer and Peter Wells' new book, Chess Improvement: It's all in the mindset)*

# Chess Olympiads: Less and Less Predictable

The breakup of the Soviet Union in the early 1990s turned the Chess Olympiad, the preeminent biennial national team championship, into a wide-open competition. What once was almost a foregone conclusion – the Soviets would capture gold and everyone else would fight for silver and bronze – now had the potential to be unpredictable.

That was nowhere more true than in the recently completed Olympiad in India. For the first time, the top three teams were all ranked outside of the top 10 at the start of the competition with the gold-medal winning team, Uzbekistan, ranked No. 14.

The charts on these two pages show the winners and their pre-tournament rankings since 1972, when rankings began. The 2020 and 2021 Olympiads, which were online and abbreviated, are not included.      *DYLAN LOEB McCLAIN*

| | 1972 | 1976* | 1978 | 1980 | 1982 | 1984 | 1986 | 1988 | 1990 | 1992 | 1994 | 1996 | |
|---|---|---|---|---|---|---|---|---|---|---|---|---|---|
| ① | Soviet Union | United States | Soviet Union | Soviet Union | Soviet Union | Soviet Union | Soviet Union | Soviet Union | Soviet Union | Russia | Russia 1 | Russia | ① |
| ② | Yugo-slavia | Argentina | Hungary | Hungary | United States | Hungary | England | England | England | England | England | England | ② |
| ③ | West Germany | Nether-lands | Yugo-slavia | Yugo-slavia | Hungary | Yugoslavia | Hungary | Hungary | United States | Ukraine | Ukraine | Hungary | ③ |
| ④ | Czecho-slavakia | *same as* Israel | United States | | Yugoslavia | England | Yugo-slavia | United States | | United States | Hungary | Ukraine | ④ |
| ⑤ | Hungary | West Germany | | | Czecho-slavakia | Czecho-slavakia | United States | Yugo-slavia | | Bosnia & Herzegovina | Germany *same as* Israel | Bulgaria *same as* Germany | ⑤ |
| ⑥ | | England | | | | Netherlands | | Iceland | | Hungary | | | ⑥ |
| ⑦ | | | | | United States | | | West Germany | | Netherlands | Netherlands | Spain | ⑦ |
| ⑧ | | | | | | | | Sweden | | Germany | Armenia | Israel | ⑧ |
| ⑨ | | | | | | | | Cuba *same as* Bulgaria | | Armenia | United States | United States | ⑨ |
| ⑩ | | | | | | | | | | Latvia | Latvia | | ⑩ |
| ⑪ | | | | | | | | Czecho-slavakia | | Georgia | Bosnia & Herzogovina | | ⑪ |
| ⑫ | | | | | | | | Netherlands | | Sweden | Russia 2 | | ⑫ |
| ⑬ | | | | | | | | | | Iceland *same as* Israel | | | ⑬ |
| ⑭ | | | | | | | | | | | | | ⑭ |
| ⑮ | | | | | | | | | | Bulgaria | | | ⑮ |
| ⑯ | | | | | | | | | | Czecho-slavakia | | | ⑯ |
| ⑰ | | | | | | | | | | Estonia | | | ⑰ |
| ⑱ | | | | | | | | | | Croatia *same as* China | | | ⑱ |
| ⑲ | | | | | | | | | | | | | ⑲ |
| ⑳ | | | | | | | | | | France | | | ⑳ |
| ㉑ | | | | | | | | | | Uzbekistan | | | ㉑ |

| | 1974 |
|---|---|
| ① | Soviet Union |
| ② | United States |
| ③ | Yugo-slavia |

*Ranking at beginning of tournament*

● Gold medal   ● Silver medal   ● Bronze medal

*In the late 1980s and throughout the 1990s, England, led by players like John Nunn and Nigel Short, boasted the second-highest ranked team in the world.*

*How deep were the Soviet teams? Imagine having to play former world champion Mikhail Tal on Board 4 in 1972.*

*Vladimir Kramnik's spectacular performance at the 1992 Olympiad when he was only 17 announced him as a player to be reckoned with.*

**Best rating performance at each Olympiad** (minimum of five games played)

| 1972 | 1974 | 1976 | 1978 | 1980 | 1982 | 1984 | 1986 | 1988 | 1990 | 1992 | 1994 | 1996 |
|---|---|---|---|---|---|---|---|---|---|---|---|---|
| **Mikhail Tal** | **Anatoly Karpov** | **Jan Timman** | **Viktor Kortchnoi** | **Jozsef Pinter** | **Anatoly Karpov** | **John Nunn** | **Garry Kasparov** | **Garry Kasparov** | **Robert Hübner** | **Vladimir Kramnik** | **Veselin Topalov** | **Garry Kasparov** |
| Board 4 | Board 1, 85,7 % | Board 1 | Board 1, 81,8 % | Reserve 2 | Board 1, 81,3 % | Board 2 | Board 1 | Board 1 | Board 1 | Reserve | Board 1 | Board 1 |
| 87,5 % | | 77,3 % | | 90,0 % | | 90,9 % | 77,3 % | 85,0 % | 70,0 % | 94,4 % | 70,8 % | 77,8 % |

*The Soviet Union and Eastern Bloc countries boycotted because it was held in Israel.

**Team medals**

| United States | Soviet Union | Yugo-slavia | Russia | Hungary | Armenia | Ukraine | England | Poland | Germany | Argen-tina | China | Czecho-slavakia | Uzbeki-stan | Israel | Sweden | Nether-lands | India | Den-mark | Bosnia & Herzo. | Bulgaria |
|---|---|---|---|---|---|---|---|---|---|---|---|---|---|---|---|---|---|---|---|---|
| 21 | 19 | 13 | 12 | 12 | 7 | 7 | 6 | 6 | 5 | 5 | 3 | 3 | 2 | 2 | 2 | 2 | 2 | 1 | 1 | 1 |
| 8 | 18 | 6 | 3 | 2 | 3 | 3 | 3 | 3 | 3 | 2 | 2 | 2 | | | | | | | | |
| 7 | | 3 | 3 | 7 | 3 | 2 | 3 | 2 | | 2 | | | | | | | | | | |
| 6 | | 6 | 6 | 3 | | 2 | | | | | | | | | | | | | | |

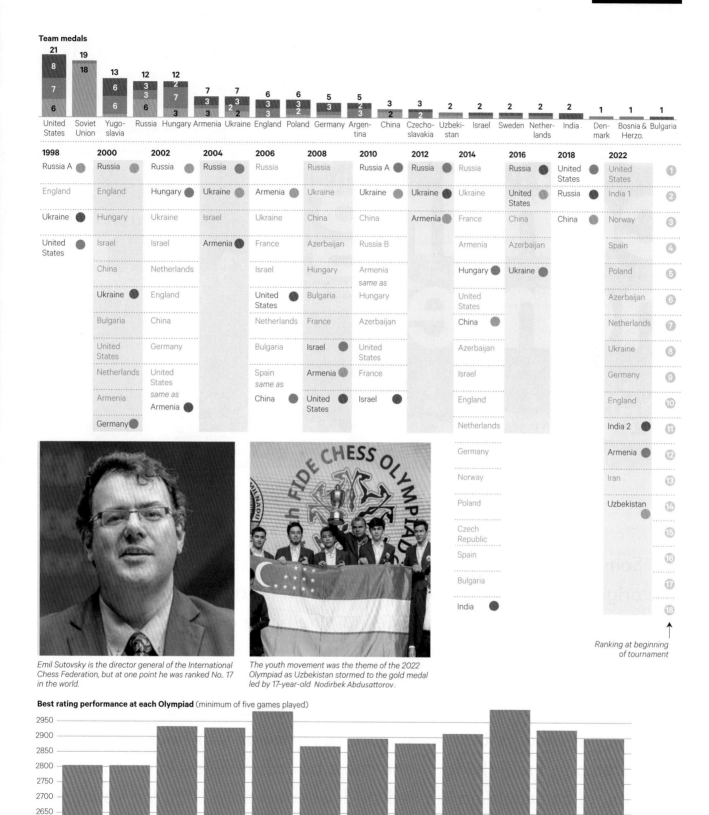

| 1998 | 2000 | 2002 | 2004 | 2006 | 2008 | 2010 | 2012 | 2014 | 2016 | 2018 | 2022 | |
|---|---|---|---|---|---|---|---|---|---|---|---|---|
| Russia A | Russia | Russia | Russia | Russia | Russia | Russia A | Russia | Russia | Russia | United States | United States | ① |
| England | England | Hungary | Ukraine | Armenia | Ukraine | Ukraine | Ukraine | Ukraine | United States | Russia | India 1 | ② |
| Ukraine | Hungary | Ukraine | Israel | Ukraine | China | China | Armenia | France | China | China | Norway | ③ |
| United States | Israel | Israel | Armenia | France | Azerbaijan | Russia B | | Armenia | Azerbaijan | | Spain | ④ |
| | China | Netherlands | | Israel | Hungary | Armenia *same as* | | Hungary | Ukraine | | Poland | ⑤ |
| | Ukraine | England | | United States | Bulgaria | Hungary | | United States | | | Azerbaijan | ⑥ |
| | Bulgaria | China | | Netherlands | France | Azerbaijan | | China | | | Netherlands | ⑦ |
| | United States | Germany | | Bulgaria | Israel | United States | | Azerbaijan | | | Ukraine | ⑧ |
| | Netherlands | United States *same as* | | Spain *same as* | Armenia | France | | Israel | | | Germany | ⑨ |
| | Armenia | Armenia | | China | United States | Israel | | England | | | England | ⑩ |
| | Germany | | | | | | | Netherlands | | | India 2 | ⑪ |
| | | | | | | | | Germany | | | Armenia | ⑫ |
| | | | | | | | | Norway | | | Iran | ⑬ |
| | | | | | | | | Poland | | | Uzbekistan | ⑭ |
| | | | | | | | | Czech Republic | | | | ⑮ |
| | | | | | | | | Spain | | | | ⑯ |
| | | | | | | | | Bulgaria | | | | ⑰ |
| | | | | | | | | India | | | | ⑱ |

*Ranking at beginning of tournament*

Emil Sutovsky is the director general of the International Chess Federation, but at one point he was ranked No.. 17 in the world.

The youth movement was the theme of the 2022 Olympiad as Uzbekistan stormed to the gold medal led by 17-year-old Nodirbek Abdusattorov.

**Best rating performance at each Olympiad** (minimum of five games played)

| 1998 | 2000 | 2002 | 2004 | 2006 | 2008 | 2010 | 2012 | 2014 | 2016 | 2018 | 2022 |
|---|---|---|---|---|---|---|---|---|---|---|---|
| Zurab Azmaiparashvili | Alexander Morozevich | Garry Kasparov | Sergey Karjakin | Bashir Al-Qudaimi | Gabriel Sargissian | Emil Sutovsky | Shakhriyar Mamedyarov | Yu Yangyi | Andrei Volokitin | Jorge Cori | David Howell |
| Board 1 | Board 2 | Board 1 | Reserve | Reserve | Board 3 | Board 2 | Board 3 | Board 3 | Reserve | Board 2 | Board 3 |
| 80,0 % | 75,0 % | 83,3 % | 92,9 % | 100 % | 81,8 % | 83,3 % | 85,0 % | 86,4 % | 94,4 % | 93,8 % | 93,8 % |

# Chess is coming home

**Young Uzbeks stun favourites to win Chennai Olympiad**

The lavish opening ceremony in the presence of Prime Minister Narendra Modi underpinned that for India the Olympiad was a symbol of national pride.

Some 1500 years after the game mysteriously and magically originated there, chess returned to India on an epic scale. In the nation's chess capital, Chennai, the home of former World Champion – and now FIDE Vice-President – Vishy Anand, teams from 186 countries gathered to celebrate the 44th Olympiad. Between a lavish opening ceremony attended by India's Prime Minister Modi and an even more spectacular four-hour closing ceremony, the fighting on the chess boards resulted in an outcome that no one could have predicted. Seeded only 14th, the youngsters of Uzbekistan took gold, ahead of Armenia and the hosts' 'junior' team, India 2. **MARIA EMELIANOVA** shares her impressions of an Olympiad that will be remembered for a long time.

The organization of the 44th Olympiad in Chennai was a massive logistic operation involving many hundreds of professionals and volunteers – an operation that miraculously was pulled off in a mere four months after the event was taken away from Moscow because of the Russian invasion of Ukraine. Olympiads are generally viewed as highlights on the chess calendar, but there was a widespread sentiment that the Chennai Olympiad was a particularly momentous and extraordinary tour de force by the All India Chess Federation.

Chennai is the capital of the state of Tamil Nadu at the very southern tip of India, and is similar in size to the entire country of Greece. India's first grandmaster and former World Champion Vishy Anand hails from Chennai (formerly known as Madras, hence his nickname 'The Tiger of Madras'), and his formidable successes have no doubt helped to make the region fertile ground for young talents. Today, Tamil Nadu boasts no fewer than 24 Grandmasters. These include some of the most recognizable and promising names in men's and women's chess, such as Praggnanandhaa, Gukesh and Pragg's sister Vaishali.

India is reputed to be a generous and hospitable nation, and this welcoming attitude and pride in the region was evident in everyone the participants encountered, at all levels of society across the region and the country. The Olympiad was also a symbol of national pride, and India's Prime Minister Narendra Modi officially opened

## India's Prime Minister Narendra Modi officially opened the Olympiad in a packed sports stadium

the Olympiad in a packed sports stadium. Besides the Prime Minister and the usual FIDE officials and dignitaries, there was also the Chief Minister of Tamil Nadu, MK Stalin – yes, named after *that* Stalin, since he was born only a few days after Josef Stalin died in 1953, and a large part of the Indian intelligentsia was sympathetic towards communism at the time.

Buses took the players to the venue and back to the hotels, but the distances were such that this could be a time-consuming affair. (MARIA EMELIANOVA/CHESS.COM)

Thambi, the mascot of the Chennai Olympiad – a half human, half horse cartoon with its hoof-hands placed in the Namaste position of welcome – was omnipresent. (MARK LIVSHITZ)

## Scorching heat

The site of the Olympiad was some 30 kilometres away from the 'centre' of Chennai, a city that covers more than 400 square kilometres and has more than 4 million inhabitants. To get an idea of the site, imagine a plot of land large enough in size for a sports stadium to comfortably sit there. On this plot of land, you have essentially a campus setting. A large modern hotel, white-walled, and with floor-to-ceiling windows, palm trees in front gently wafting in the breeze and a sapphire-brilliant blue sky. Frankly, the building wouldn't look out of place in a swanky district of the Algarve or the French Riviera.

In front of the hotel there was a surprisingly green and soft lawn – surprising because the temperature is an almost constant 30 Celsius or higher and the sun is always scorching. Yet, the grass stays resiliently green with no sign of yellowing or dryness.

On the other side of this palm-tree bordered lawn sat a large, rather boring and plain-looking rectangular building. Any type of mundane corporate activity could be imagined in this functional but architecturally thoughtless building. This was the concrete-column conference centre where most of the matches were played. Not far away from it was an identical clone of this building, albeit in a setting which was less green and had more asphalt. This was the second conference centre, where the remainder of the games were played.

## Pashminas

With such unrelenting heat, naturally the buildings had to be air-conditioned. In fact the air-conditioning was so strong that many players actually felt cold. Some players were so wrapped up in coats and jackets that you wouldn't be able to tell that they were playing in tropical conditions.

To fight the extreme differences in temperature, I had purchased several pashminas of remarkable quality. My temperature was kept cool in the heat and comfortably warm in the cold, thanks to the Changthangi goats that provide the pashmina wool, a type of wool that is even finer than cashmere. This fabric, produced by simple methods that have been known for hundreds if not thousands of years, fared far better in the humidity than modern equipment and synthetic fibres.

But the extreme temperature differences remained a challenge. Every time I left the playing hall, I had a small heart attack as the most expensive possessions I had with me – my camera lenses – would fog up and I would be terrified of the sensitive electronics within the lens and my camera being damaged. I would have loved to be advised on this problem by photographers who are used to working in tropical climates!

Close to the conference centre, a hotel acted like the heart of the complex, with pale yellow patios sprawled outwards like some nervous system. These patios naturally connected everything together, but also led to some very nice villas surrounded by lush and leafy tropical vegetation. However, the majority of the teams were not staying in this hotel or its villas; it had long ago been booked out by the small army of the All India Chess Federation and the FIDE officials required to run and organize such an event. Most of the teams and players had to come from hotels further afield, some of them up to 50 kilometres away. Transportation with buses was provided, with players generally not having to wait any more than 20 minutes after their game had ended, but the distances were such that this could be a time-consuming affair. While not ideal for the players with a long commute each way, in fairness to the organizers it must be kept in mind that they had taken on the Olympiad with only months to prepare, after the hosting rights were withdrawn from Russia on the basis of an IOC recommendation following their act of war against Ukraine.

The long distances between the hotels not only meant a tiring commute for the players; they also limited the possibilities of a social life. At most Olympiads, players generally stay in hotels within walking distance of each other, so they can meet and

**The passion and unbridled enthusiasm of the fans was overwhelming and could only be described as chess mania.** (MARIA EMELIANOVA/CHESS.COM)

**That's what you got when Vishy Anand entered the room… If you look carefully you may catch a glimpse of the former World Champion.** (MARIA EMELIANOVA/CHESS.COM)

hang out with old and new friends every day. This element of 'gens una sumus' is an important part of Olympiads, and it was a pity that this time, meeting other players was virtually impossible if they did not stay in the same hotel.

Another reality was that the coronavirus was still around, even though many people prefer to treat it as a distant memory. During the Olympiad, India was seeing a modest rise in reported cases of Covid-19, but anecdotal evidence seemed to indicate that in reality the number of unreported cases were rampant. Dozens of players and officials came down with Covid-19 or with symptoms remarkably similar to it (but dismissed as a cold/flu and a refusal to test).

FIDE has seen Covid-19 break out at every event it has held since the 2020 Candidates Tournament in Yekaterinburg was aborted. Yet they are struggling to learn from their mistakes and fail to implement clear processes and procedures in terms of reporting outbreaks, efforts at contact-tracing, and messaging of individuals. It seems as if FIDE would prefer to ignore the risks and make it, in the words of Douglas Adams, an 'SEP' or 'someone else's problem'.

### Chess mania

The interest in the Olympiad, regionally and nationally, went far beyond anything we have been used to in chess. The passion and unbridled enthusiasm was so overwhelming that I was reminded of stories I was told as a child, about the pride and joy everyone felt in the USSR whenever major chess events were going on in Moscow. If we are are talking about 'chess mania', it seems that at this moment India truly deserves the top spot for fanaticism about chess.

Everything everywhere had a chess theme. Bus stops, walls all over and around Mahabalipuram, advertising in stores, even cartons of milk and desserts were chess-themed. Chess was impossible to avoid – everyone knew about the Olympiad, and random people in stores would ask

## Bus stops, walls all over and around Mahabalipuram, advertising in stores, even cartons of milk and desserts were chess-themed

you about the chess and which players were your favourite. Even the local bridge – the Napier Bridge – caused controversy by being covered top to bottom in a chequered black-and-white board theme. The controversy as to whether it was a risk to drivers or not received national attention with an article in the *Times of India.*

Thambi, the Bojack-horseman styled mascot of the Chennai Olympiad – a half human, half horse cartoon with its hoof-hands placed in the *Namaste* position of welcome – was omnipresent. A giant Thambi statue greeted all arrivals at the airport. A different Thambi greeted guests at the hotels. A slightly terrifying family of Thambis, as if saying 'join us, become like us' – father, mother, daughter and son – greeted players and visitors alike at the playing hall. Much like chess, Thambi was everywhere, and everyone knew Thambi. Actually, it would be unsurprising to learn that Thambi can travel through space and time, and manipulate matter to manifest itself in all sorts of sizes and shapes. It wouldn't surprise me if, after arriving home, all players and officials – not just the medal winners – somehow had their own personal Thambis welcoming them back as they crossed their own thresholds.

### Tragedy

And who could blame anyone for getting swept up by chess mania? With such an abundance of shocking and staggering results? Who could have imagined that the odds-on

**The dramatic key moment of the 44th Olympiad. Gukesh cannot believe his blunder and Nodirbek Abdusattorov cannot believe his luck.** (LENNART OOTES)

**The closing ceremony was even more spectacular than the opening night and lasted for more than four hours.** (LENNART OOTES)

favourites of Team USA would struggle and even fail to reach the podium? Or that Norway, seeded 3rd and led by World Champion Magnus Carlsen (who performed well on Board 1, scoring 7½/9 and winning bronze) would be relegated to the second playing hall and end in 59th (!) place?

For the Indian fans, the narrative woven in particular by the India 2 team appeared like something out of a fairy-tale. India 2 and Gukesh in particular were on fire, with the Board 1 player blasting away with a streak of eight straight wins.

Uzbekistan and India 2 – two extremely young teams – were the sensations of the Chennai Olympiad. The average age of both teams was approx. 22 and 19 respectively – with the vast majority being under 20, plus one 'veteran' player each (27-year-old Jakhongir Vakhidov, with a 2813 performance, and 29-year-old Adhiban, scoring 6/10) to steady the ship. The two teams clashed in Round 9, when Uzbekistan was topping the table and India 2 was one match point behind. It was impossible not to see their clash as the battle of India's new generation versus the new generation of Uzbekistan.

Things looked gloomy for Uzbekistan, as India 2 seemed to be steering for a 3-1 victory, with Gukesh having a totally winning position against Uzbekistan's star player, Rapid World Champion Nodirbek Abdusattorov.

The atmosphere was electrifying as the two young lions battled it out. Abdusattorov tried to hang in and was rewarded for his tenacity when Gukesh let his advantage slip through his fingers. And then a tragedy unfolded, when Gukesh spurned the draw that would have brought his team victory and kept playing for a win. And when there was no longer a way to force a draw, he blundered horribly.

**Gukesh D**
**Nodirbek Abdusattorov**
Chennai Olympiad 2022 (10)

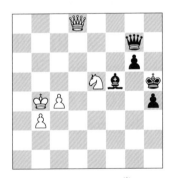

position after 71...♕g7

Defending a slightly worse endgame, White should have defended the attacked knight with the queen, for example 72.♕d5 (or first a check on d1), but in one move he ruined a beautiful dream.
**72.♘f3** A terrible oversight that loses the knight. **72...♕b7+** And a devastated Gukesh, unable to do anything, lost on time.

**Chevrolet Equinox SUV**

With this bizarre turnaround, Abdusattorov saved the match for his team as they levelled the score 2-2. That improbable save essentially decided the Olympiad. Suddenly the fairy-tale of India 2 had become the fairy-tale of Uzbekistan. Now they knew that if they defeated the Netherlands in the final round, they would be Olympiad champions.

And that is what they duly did, 2½-1½, watched by the president of the Uzbek Chess Federation, Alisher Sadullaev, who has done so much to develop and fund chess in his country. Humbly and quietly watching, he gave no fist pumps, slapped no backs. Yet for all of the last three rounds he watched his boys play, hardly leaving the playing hall and showing no interest in anything other than the games.

Their improbable success did not go unnoticed in their home country either. On their return, the players were received and rewarded like heroes. Each member of the team received the equivalent of 53,000 euros plus a Chevrolet Equinox SUV.

Armenia finished in second place, living up to their reputation of being Olympiad specialists. They collected the same number of match points as Uzbekistan, but the tiebreak unequivocally relegated the Armenians to the silver medals. Now that Levon Aronian has moved to the United States, Gabriel Sargissian played on Board 1, once again pulling off an outstanding Olympiad performance.

India 2 finished the tournament with a 3-1 win over Germany and collected the bronze medals. A great result, but how could they be unreservedly happy, knowing that gold had been within reach?

The Indian fans kept their contagious enthusiasm till the very last days, and the Indian press kept turning up in improbable numbers. Honestly speaking, I have never seen such media attention for a chess event before – or such public interest, for that matter, with the possible exception of some days during a World Championship. But even there, it was rarely as sustained and unflagging as at this Olympiad.

The massive press interest also created challenges. The numbers were so great that the various levels of accreditation were not always

## A great result for India 2, but how could they be unreservedly happy, knowing that gold had been within reach?

clear to the volunteers. Sometimes queues to get through security or pass through the various halls were long or a bit of a squeeze. Yet, these issues were minor, and undoubtedly a small price to pay for such significant interest in the game we all love so much. In fact, the chess world can only hope that it will continue. India, after all, is the birthplace of the board game that chess has probably evolved from. In the slightly adapted words of the English football fans, it was tempting to say 'Chess is coming home!'

## Olympiad Selection

With literally thousands of games having been played, it is totally impossible to give full coverage of the Olympiad, or even to present a representative selection. But you can make carefully considered choices. Elsewhere in this issue, Jan Timman looks at a number of the stars of this edition, while Judit Polgar gives examples of players of lesser fame who got a chance to shine. And of course there is a special article on the Women's Olympiad, that was won by Ukraine.

Below, we present a choice of the absolute highlights from the Open section. Great games that will be remembered, annotated by the stars of this Olympiad. Games that are a joy to play through, and that contain many lessons.

**Nodirbek Abdusattorov**, the leader of the winning team from Uzbekistan, presents two key games: his win against Fabiano Caruana and the draw in the last round against Anish Giri.

**Hrant Melkumyan** played a prominent role on the silver Armenian team, turning in a 2713 performance on Board 2, and showcases his favourite win.

Needless to say, the star of the sensational India 2 team and the winner of the gold medal on Board 1 is also there. The amazing **Gukesh** comments on the two games that he was most proud of, his splendid wins against Shirov and Sargissian.

Two more members of India 2 analyse the game they liked best. Board 2 **Nihal Sarin** (TPR 2774!) shows a flashy win against Switzerland, and Board 4 'veteran' **Adhiban** dissects a win that helped his team defeat Spain.

We round off with an instructive win of our contributing editor **Anish Giri**. Anish had the fifth result on Board 1, with a 2795 performance, and won a delightful attacking game against Georgia's top board Baadur Jobava.

NOTES BY
**Nodirbek Abdusattorov**

**Fabiano Caruana**
**Nodirbek Abdusattorov**
Chennai Olympiad 2022 (4)
Queen's Pawn Opening, London System

In Round 4, we played against the tournament favourites, team USA. We knew that it would be a tough match and that if we wanted to fight for the medals, we would have to overcome them. Therefore our team was fully focused. My opponent was Fabiano Caruana. This was my first classical game against him, although we have played many rapid games online. Obviously, my strategy was to play solid chess, and a draw was considered a good result for our match strategy.
**1.d4 d5 2.♗f4**

A surprise! I was not ready to play against the London System, and I took my time to choose from many lines.
**2...♘f6 3.e3 c5 4.♘f3 ♘c6 5.♘bd2 cxd4 6.exd4 ♗f5**
6...♗g4 was my choice against Praggnanandhaa in the 2021 Grand Swiss.
**7.♗b5 ♕b6 8.c4 dxc4 9.a4 ♗d3!?**
9...e6 has been a more regular choice.
**10.♘e5 e6**

**11.♕f3?!** This looks tempting, but it gives Black an extra tempo.

11.♘dxc4 should have been played, e.g. 11...♗b4+ 12.♗d2 ♗xd2+ 13.♕xd2 ♗xc4 14.♘xc4 ♕c7 15.♘e5 0-0 16.♖c1 ♘e4 17.♕e3 ♕a5+ 18.♔e2 ♘f6 19.♘xc6 bxc6 20.♗xc6 ♖ab8 21.b3 ♖fd8, and Black has sufficient compensation for the pawn.

**11...♖c8**

**12.♘xd3**

It was obvious that something had gone wrong for my opponent, and at this point I felt very confident.

Maybe 12.d5 was the idea behind 11.♕f3, but it doesn't work: 12...♘xd5! 13.♘xf7 ♗b4 14.♘xh8 ♕d4!, and Black is winning: 15.♗e3 ♕xb2.

**12...cxd3 13.♕xd3 a6**

13...♘d5!? was a good alternative.

**14.♘c4 ♗b4+ 15.♗d2 ♗xd2+ 16.♕xd2 ♕c7 17.♗xc6+ ♕xc6 18.♘e3 0-0 19.0-0**

**19...♘e4?!**

19...♕b6! was much stronger, when after 20.♖fc1? (or 20.♖fd1 ♖fd8, and Black is better in view of the vulnerability of the d4-pawn) 20...♘e4! is the point, and Black is winning.

**20.♕b4 ♖fd8 21.a5**

**21...♘d6?!** My idea was to transfer my knight to b5, but I had underestimated the coming pawn sacrifice. 21...♖c7!, followed by ...♖cd7, was very strong. **22.♖fd1 ♘b5 23.d5!**

With this pawn sac White gets enough counterplay.

**23...exd5 24.♘f5 ♕c5**

24...♔h8!? was an interesting alternative: 25.♘e7 ♕c4! 26.♘xd5 g6 27.♕xc4 ♖xc4, and Black is slightly better.

**25.♕h4** 25.♕g4! was better: 25...♕f8 (25...g6 26.♖e1) 26.h4, with compensation for the pawn.

**25...f6 26.♕g4**

**26...g6?** A missed opportunity. 26...♖c7! would have yielded an almost decisive advantage: 27.h4

(27.♖e1 ♕c4 28.♕g3 d4, and Black is winning) 27...♕c4! 28.♕g3 d4 29.♖d2 ♕c5 30.♕g4 g6, and Black is very much calling the shots.

**27.♘d4**

Now White blocks the pawn and has good counterplay with h4-h5.

**27...♘xd4 28.♖xd4 ♔f7 29.h4 ♕b5 30.♖e1 ♖e8 31.♖ed1 ♖c4 32.♖xc4 dxc4**

At this point I was very confident about my winning chances. I'm up a

Top board Nodirbek Abdusattorov led Uzbekistan to a historic result, outshining the silver medals that were won at the 1992 Olympiad in Manila.

♕g5 50.♖b6 White is even a tad better) 45.♕xb7 gxf2 46.♖xh7+ ♔g5 47.♕g7+ ♔g6 48.♕xg6+ ♔xg6 49.♖a7, and this should be a draw.
**44...♖h4!**

Now the game is just over. White is lost.
**45.♔xg3 ♖h5 46.♕f4+ ♕g5+ 47.♕g4 ♕xg4+ 48.♔xg4 ♖g5+!**

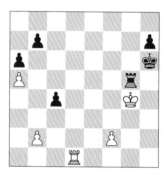

The last accurate move. The rest is easy.
**49.♔f4 ♖xa5 50.♖d6+ ♔h5 51.♖d7 ♖b5 52.♖xh7+ ♔g6 53.♖c7 ♖xb2 54.♔e5 b5 55.♖c6+ ♔h5 56.f4 a5 57.f5 a4 58.♖c8 a3 59.♖h8+ ♔g5 60.♖g8+ ♔h6 61.f6 ♖f2**

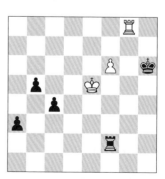

White resigned.

---

pawn after all. But the engine, much to my surprise, assesses the position as 0.00!

**33.h5?!** More to the point was 33.♕d4!?. My king is weak and this is what counts most in this position. 33...♖e7 34.♕d8, and this should be a draw.
**33...gxh5! 34.♕f4 ♔g6 35.♕c7 ♖e4 36.♕c8 ♖e8 37.♕c7 ♖e4 38.♕c8 ♕b4**

**39.♔h2** After 39.♕g8+ ♔h6 it is impossible to understand over the board that 40.♕h8! is strong: 40...♖f4 (40...♕xb2 41.♕f8+ ♔g6 42.♕g8+, with a draw; 40...♕e7?? even loses: 41.♖d7! ♖e1+ 42.♔h2 ♕e5+ 43.g3) 41.g3 ♖f5 42.♕g8, with a draw.

**39...♕e7! 40.g3 h4 41.♕g8+ ♔h6 42.♔g2 f5 43.♕c8! hxg3**

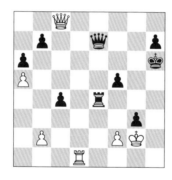

**44.♕xf5??** Missing a cool rook manoeuvre. 44.♖d7! was an absolute must: 44...♕e8 (maybe my opponent had missed that after 44...♕f6?! he

## 'I'm up a pawn. But the engine, much to my surprise, assesses the position as 0.00!'

has 45.♖xb7!, with the threat ♖b6, and after 45...♖e6 46.♕xc4 ♔h5 47.♕f4 h6 48.♕f3+ ♔g6 49.♕xg3+

NOTES BY
**Nodirbek Abdusattorov**

**Nodirbek Abdusattorov
Anish Giri**
Chennai Olympiad 2022 (11)
Sicilian Defence, Najdorf Defence

This game was played in the final round of the Olympiad, when we were facing the strong team of the Netherlands. Going into the last round, we were in the lead, together with the Armenian team. We were expecting Armenia to win their match against Spain, so we had to win our match in order to secure the gold medals, as we had a far better tiebreak in case of a tie.

My opponent was the well-known Super GM Anish Giri. I played him in the 2021 World Cup in Sochi, where I was able to eliminate him in a rapid play-off.

The final round was played in the morning, so I preferred to save energy and tried to sleep well instead of doing prep.

**1.e4 c5** I was a bit surprised by this choice, as I had been expecting the more solid 1...e5.

**2.♘f3 d6 3.d4 cxd4 4.♘xd4 ♘f6
5.♘c3 a6 6.♖g1**

A rare sub-line that has been played many times by Ian Nepomniachtchi, even against Anish himself.

**6...h5** A very principled approach. Calmer positions arise after 6...e5.

**7.h3 g6 8.♗e3 ♗g7**

Already a novelty! But maybe 8...b5 was better.

**9.♕e2 b5 10.0-0-0 ♘bd7**

**11.g4** Here, 11.f4! would have posed big problems for Black early on:
– 11...e5 12.♘c6 ♕c7 13.♘b4!, and White is clearly better. One of the knights will find a great square on d5 and White can work on a kingside attack by aiming to push g4.
– 11...♗b7 would run into 12.e5! dxe5 13.fxe5 ♘d5 14.♘xd5 ♗xd5 15.g4! ♘xe5 16.♗g2 e6 17.gxh5 ♖xh5 18.♘xe6! fxe6 19.♗xd5 exd5 20.♖xg6 ♖h7 21.♕g2!, and White wins. Of course, these are all engine lines, but it shows how quickly Black can end up in a lost position.

**11...♗b7 12.♗g2** Threatening e5.

**12...b4 13.♘d5 e5! 14.♘xf6+**
14.♘b3!? was an interesting alternative.
**14...♘xf6 15.♘b3 ♕c7 16.gxh5**
16.♔b1 0-0 17.f4 was also an option.

**16...♘xh5** I had underestimated 16...♖xh5!, as Black will not able to castle. But he has very good attacking chances on the queenside: 17.♔b1 a5 18.♕b5+ ♗c6 19.♗b6 ♕d7 20.♕d3 ♕b7! 21.♗xa5 ♖xe4, with complicated play.

**17.♕d2**
A double attack on b4 and d6.

**17...♖c8**
The correct move order was 17...♘f4! 18.♗f3 a5 19.♕xd6 ♕xd6 20.♖xd6 ♖xh3 21.♗g4 ♖h8, with an equal position.

**18.♔b1 ♘f4 19.♗f3!**

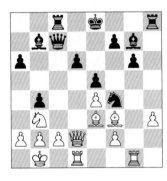

Now this is possible, as White can play ♗g4.
**19...0-0** Taking the pawn, 19...♘xh3, is a bad idea: 20.♖h1 ♘f4 21.♖xh8+ ♗xh8 22.♕xd6! ♕xc2+ 23.♔a1 ♕c6 24.♘a5 ♕xd6 25.♖xd6, and White should be winning.

**20.♕xb4**
20.♔a1! was even stronger.
**20...d5!**

**21.c3!**
This poses good practical problems. The engines prefer 21.♖d2!?. I thought that this would be far easier to play for Black, for example

21...♘xh3 22.♖h1 d4 23.♖xh3 dxe3 24.fxe3 ♖fd8, but this is clearly better for White.

**21...dxe4?!**

This gives White good chances. Instead, 21...d4! was a strong sacrifice to open up my king: 22.cxd4 exd4, and now, after 23.♘xd4 ♖b8! 24.♘b3 ♖fc8, the position is not so clear.

**22.♗xe4 ♗xe4+ 23.♕xe4 ♘xh3 24.♖ge1**

Now White has a pleasant advantage, thanks to his passed pawns on the queenside.

**24...♘f4 25.♘c5**

A very interesting option was 25.♗xf4!? exf4 26.♕a4!, threatening ♖d7 and ♕xa6. This was the move that I had missed.

**25...♕c6 26.♗xf4 exf4?!**

26...♕xe4+! was a much better version: 27.♘xe4 exf4 28.♔c2 ♖fe8 29.a4 ♖e5, and Black should be fine.

**27.♕xc6 ♖xc6 28.♖d5! ♖fc8 29.♘d3**

This should be winning for White, as his rooks and knight dominate all the good squares.

**29...♗f6 30.♖g1! ♖b6 31.♔c2 ♖c4**

**32.♖e1?**

A strange oversight. 32.♖f5!! just wins the pawn, but for some reason it didn't come to my mind: 32...♗h4 33.♖g2, and the f-pawn will drop off.

**32...♔g7 33.♖c5?!**

After 33.f3 g5 White is slightly better.

**33...♖xc5 34.♘xc5 ♗h4**

Now it's unclear, because Black has enough counterplay. In the remaining moves I decided to play it safe, so as not to worry my team mates.

**35.♘d3 g5 36.c4 ♔f6 37.b4 f3 38.c5 ♖e6 39.♔d1 g4 40.a4 g3 41.fxg3 ♗xg3 42.♖f1 ♖e3 43.♔d2 ♖e2+**

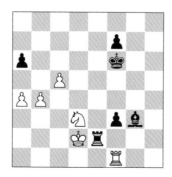

**44.♔d1 ♖e3 45.♔d2 ♖e2+ 46.♔d1**
Draw.

NOTES BY
**Hrant Melkumyan**

# 'Second place was a great achievement for Armenia, and I am extremely proud of my team's efforts'

**Valentin Dragnev**
**Hrant Melkumyan**
Chennai Olympiad 2022 (4)
Caro-Kann, Advance Variation

My general impression of the Olympiad was that the organization was extremely smooth and I would struggle to suggest a way the tournament could have been improved upon. The enthusiasm shown by the volunteers and everyone involved was contagious and motivated me to play well. It is a special feeling to have such great appreciation from the fans.

Perhaps one interesting consideration for future Olympiads would be a review of the tie-break system. It was quite spectacular that Armenia led the tournament for the majority of the event, but was never really in contention for a strong tie-break, despite playing the strongest teams. In any case, second place was a great achievement for my country, and I am extremely proud of my team's efforts. The experience was unforgettable and something I will treasure for the remainder of my life.

**1.e4 c6** Going in to the Olympiad, my intention was to stick with the Caro-Kann, because it is a solid opening that leads to lots of interesting positions (I also refer to my game against Wesley So – And this is what he is referring to – ed.:

So-Melkumyan
Chennai Olympiad 2022 (7)
position after 18.♗h6

With his last move, Wesley So allowed 18...e4, and only after 19.♖xe4 Hrant Melkumyan realized that the pawn had been heavily poisoned and played 19...♘f8 (as after 19...dxe4, 20.♕xf7+! spectacularly leads to mate: 20...♔xf7 21.♗c4+ ♔f6 22.♘xe4+ ♔f5 23.g4+ ♔xe4 24.♖e1+ ♔f3 25.♖e3 mate). Now Black lost after 20.♖f4 f5 21.♘xf5 gxf5 22.♖xf5 ♕d6 23.♕g4+ ♘g6 24.♖xd5 ♕f6 25.g3 ♗f8 26.♖f5 ♕e7 27.♗c4+ ♔h8 28.♖g5 1-0).
**2.d4 d5 3.e5 ♗f5 4.h4**

This move is quite popular nowadays. White's main plan is to use the space advantage obtained with the pawn on e5.
**4...h5 5.♗d3 ♗xd3 6.♕xd3 ♕a5+**
6...e6 is another main line, but White seems to get a slight edge.
**7.♘d2**
7.b4 is an interesting pawn sacrifice, which that leads to lots of unusual positions after 7...♕xb4+ 8.♘d2 e6 9.♖b1 ♕e7.
**7...e6 8.♘gf3 ♘h6 9.0-0 ♘f5 10.a4**

Continuing with the idea to obtain a space advantage, but now on the queenside.
**10...♘d7** 10...♗e7 is more accurate, but I mixed up some of my preparation and thought 10...♘d7 was best.
**11.♘b3 ♕a6 12.♕d1**
The endgame after 12.♕xa6?! bxa6 is very comfortable for Black.
**12...c5 13.dxc5 ♘xc5**
13...♗xc5 is a more accurate move, as it allows for faster development, which is crucial when you are behind in development.
**14.♘bd4 ♘xd4 15.♘xd4**

Typically this structure slightly favours White. While Black's position is solid, White has more space to manoeuvre their pieces and Black is a bit passive.
**15...♖c8 16.♖e1 ♕b6 17.c3 a6 18.g3 g6 19.♔g2 ♗g7 20.a5 ♕c7 21.♗f4 ♘d7**

After a series of moves to bolster my position, it is finally time to reposi-

Armenia's second board Hrant Melkumyan felt inspired to play well by the enthusiasm shown by the volunteers and everyone involved in the Chennai Olympiad.

tion my knight. While the knight may seem well placed on c5, it is not doing much and will have better placement on c6. If you have a passive position, you are generally happy to exchange pieces, as this will open up the board and allow for greater mobility of your pieces.

**22.♘f3 ♘b8 23.b4 ♘c6**

**24.♖c1?!**
Following 23.b4, White needed to play 24.♗e3 and ♗b6. In the current position, c4 is weak for no reason.
The position after 24.♗e3!? ♘xe5 25.♗b6 ♘xf3 (25...♕d6?? is a blunder: 26.♘xe5 ♗xe5 27.♖xe5 ♕xe5 28.♗d4 ♕e4+ 29.f3, and White wins) 26.♖xe6+ fxe6 27.♗xc7 ♘xh4+ 28.gxh4 ♖xc7 is hard to evaluate, but it looks like a risky situation and

Black would need to play accurately to hold.
**24...♘e7**

Once Black has castled, the knight on e7 is well placed to move to f5 and prevent a lot of white attacking chances connected with ♘g5 and g4.
**25.♕d2 ♕d7 26.♗g5 ♖c4 27.♕d3 0-0 28.♘d2**

The rook on c4 is preventing all of White's play, so it needs to be pushed away.
**28...♖c7 29.♘b3 ♖fc8 30.♕d2**
After 30.♘c5 Black can choose between sacrificing the exchange with 30...♖xc5 31.bxc5 ♖xc5 and going 30...♕b5.
**30...♖c4**

**31.♘d4?** This is a crucial mistake. After this move, White has few counter-chances.
31.♘c5 was necessary, after which Black has several ways to get a comfortable position. He can either sacrifice the exchange or play ...♕c7.
**31...♘c6 32.♘f3 ♕c7 33.♗f4 ♘e7 34.♗g5 ♘f5**

Now Black's pieces have achieved close to maximum activity and it's time to start breaking through. At this point, the match score was 1-1 and both of us had a few minutes on the clock. Meanwhile, my teammate's position was worrisome. Rather than break through immediately, I played cautiously to reach the time-control, and determine the appropriate course of action later.
**35.♕a2 ♗f8** I had completely

missed 35...♗h6!, which would have been extremely strong. This would have allowed me to capture the c3-pawn without any issues.

35...♖xc3 is impossible, in view of 36.♖xc3 ♕xc3 37.♖c1.

**36.♗d2 ♗e7 37.♕b1 ♖g4 38.♘h2**

The only move.

**38...♖c4** 38...♕c4 39.♘xg4 ♕xg4 also seems to work for Black, but I didn't want to force things just yet.

**39.♘f3 ♕d7 40.♖cd1 ♕b5 41.♖c1 ♔g7 42.♕a1?**

With the queen on a1, all of the tactics start working for Black.

**42...♖g4 43.♘h2 ♘xh4+ 44.♔h1 ♕d3! 45.♖cd1**

Threatening ♗h6+, to win the queen.

**45...♕f5!**

| Chennai (open) 2022 | | |
|---|---|---|
| | Pts | Tiebreak |
| 1 Uzbekistan | 19 | 435 |
| 2 Armenia | 19 | 382.5 |
| 3 India 2 | 18 | 427.5 |
| 4 India | 17 | 409 |
| 5 USA | 17 | 352 |
| 6 Moldova | 17 | 316.5 |
| 7 Azerbaijan | 16 | 351.5 |
| 8 Hungary | 16 | 341.5 |
| 9 Poland | 16 | 322.5 |
| 10 Lithuania | 16 | 297 |
| 11 Netherlands | 15 | 362.5 |
| 12 Spain | 15 | 356.5 |
| 13 France | 15 | 353 |
| 14 England | 15 | 348.5 |
| 15 Greece | 15 | 331 |
| 16 Israel | 15 | 326 |
| 17 Kazakhstan | 15 | 322.5 |
| 18 Germany | 15 | 321 |
| 19 Cuba | 15 | 319 |
| 20 Serbia | 15 | 315.5 |
| 21 Brazil | 15 | 306 |
| 22 Montenegro | 15 | 299 |
| 23 Austria | 15 | 283.5 |
| 24 Peru | 15 | 278 |
| 25 Czech Republic | 14 | 352.5 |
| 26 Iran | 14 | 334.5 |
| 27 Georgia | 14 | 334 |
| 28 Turkey | 14 | 333.5 |
| 29 Ukraine | 14 | 326.5 |
| 30 Australia | 14 | 319.5 |
| 31 India 3 | 14 | 311.5 |
| 32 Philippines | 14 | 305.5 |
| 33 Argentina | 14 | 299.5 |
| 34 Indonesia | 14 | 298.5 |
| 35 Mongolia | 14 | 297.5 |
| 36 Egypt | 14 | 284.5 |
| 37 Sweden | 14 | 275.5 |
| 38 Chile | 14 | 275 |
| 39 Slovakia | 14 | 269 |
| 40 Iceland | 14 | 254.5 |
| **188 teams, 11 rounds** | | |

The only winning move. The queen connects to the attack, lending it deadly force.

**46.gxh4 ♕xf2**

Here White resigned. Had he continued, the game could have ended the following way: 47.♘xg4 hxg4 48.♖f1 ♕xh4+ 49.♔g2 ♕h3+ 50.♔f2 ♕f3+ 51.♔g1 ♕g3+ 52.♔h1 ♖h8+ 53.♗h6+ ♖xh6 mate.

NOTES BY
**Gukesh D**

**Alexei Shirov**
**Gukesh D**
Chennai Olympiad 2022 (5)
Sicilian Defence

This game was played in Round 5. I was on 4/4, so I was in a good form. My opponent is obviously one of the greatest attackers of the game and my strategy was to just try to provoke him into making some aggressive moves and use my chances.

**1.e4** This was expected, as he mostly plays 1.e4 and there was no chance he would play anything else, because I play the Sicilian. ☺

**1...c5 2.♘f3 ♘c6 3.♘c3 e5 4.♗c4**

**4...d6** After 4...♗e7 5.d3 d6 6.0-0 h6 7.♘d5 ♘f6 8.c3 0-0 9.a3 ♘xd5 10.♗xd5 ♗f6 I got a normal position, but ended up losing in Navara-Gukesh, Riga 2021.

**5.d3 h6**

This is an interesting move order, with its pros and cons. I thought it would be a surprise for him, as I had played a few games against strong opponents with 4...♗e7.

**6.♘d5**

I had not expected this. 6.0-0 would have been a natural move, but Shirov is true to his style: in retrospect I can say that he was probably already thinking about ♖g1 ideas, as I have already played ...h6. But I did not understand it during the game, and probably for good reasons.

**6...♘f6 7.c3** He wants either a quick b4 or something that I was not expecting, which was ♖g1 and g4. After 7.♘xf6+ ♕xf6 8.c3 I wanted something like 8...♗e7 9.0-0 ♕g6.

**7...♗e7 8.a3 a5**

It would feel as if I'm strategically worse, as I have already given up both the d5- and the b5-squares. But the point is that it is not easy for White to exploit these weaknesses, as I'm already challenging the d5-square and he needs his other knight to be on the kingside. If he tries to get the knight to b5, I can take some action on the kingside with ...f5

**9.♖g1?!** This is not a great idea, even though it is Shirov who's playing it. After I recovered from the initial shock of seeing his move, I was quite happy, since I just knew that it couldn't be great. I have made some strategic concessions, but I have not

## 'This is not a great idea, even though it is Shirov who's playing it'

There were no strict anti-Covid guidelines, and officially no cases were reported, but that did not stop Gukesh from taking precautionary measures.

compromised my king at all, so there surely can't be any attack.
9.a4 0-0 would have been the normal way for play to continue.

**9...♘xd5**

I played the following moves quite quickly, as I thought that this was the most natural way to play and I couldn't see anything wrong with it. 9...0-0 would be playing into White's hands.

**10.♗xd5** After 10.exd5 the retreat 10...♘b8 is fine for me.

**10...♗e6**

**11.♗xe6**
After 11.g4 Black will continue 11...♕d7.

**11...fxe6 12.g4 ♕d7 13.g5 hxg5 14.♗xg5 ♗xg5 15.♖xg5 0-0-0**

I had seen this position when playing 9...♘xd5, and I thought I would have no problems here. I was confident that this should be good, as I was making all the natural moves.

**16.♕e2** He must have realized that there was no attack now.
16.b4?, to capitalize on my slight expansion, does not work: 16...♖df8 17.bxc5 ♕f7 18.♖g3 ♖xh2.

**16...♖df8 17.0-0-0 ♖f7**

I was wondering if I should play ...♖f7 right away or fix the queenside with ...a4 first, but realized it didn't make a difference.

**18.♖g2**

Protecting the f2-pawn to free his knight.

18.a4? stops ...a4, but as the queen is busy protecting the knight of f3, White cannot allow the position to be opened up: 18...♘a7! 19.b3 b5 20.axb5 ♘xb5 21.♔b2 ♖hf8 22.♖g3 ♕b7, and Black is winning.

**18...a4**

Now it's probably time.

**19.♖dg1**

I am not sure what the purpose of this move is, but it's hard to find something to do for White anyway.

After 19.♘d2 Black proceeds with 19... b5.

**19...b5!?** This was an interesting decision, as I saw there was a possibility for White to complicate the game with ♘g5 and d4. I saw the next moves till 28...♘a5 and I evaluated the position correctly.

**20.♘g5 ♖e7 21.d4?**

Objectively this is bad, but I had been expecting it, because I felt Shirov would be very uncomfortable to just sit and wait, as there is nothing else to do.

**21...exd4   22.♕xb5   ♘e5**
**23.♕a6+ ♕b7**

**24.♕xb7+**

24.♕xd6 loses to 24...♘d3+ 25.♔c2 ♖d8.
**24...♔xb7 25.cxd4 cxd4 26.♖d1**

**26...♘c6** I found the position after 26...♘g6!? 27.♖xd4 ♘f4 a beautiful one, as White cannot escape a knight fork, even though he can give check! But White has good drawing chances after 28.♖b4+ ♔c6 29.♖c4+ ♔b5 30.♖b4+ ♔a5 31.♖g3 ♘e2+ 32.♔d2 ♘xg3 33.hxg3.
**27.f4 e5!** I knew this move would allow f5 and ♘e6, with some threats to my g7-pawn, but I felt that with my knight on b3 there should be stronger threats.
I would prefer to play 27...♘a5 without allowing f5 and ♘e6, but then 28.e5 would be a problem.

**28.f5 ♘a5 29.♘e6 ♘b3+ 30.♔b1**

**30...♔b6!**
I was very happy to find this move. Maybe there are stronger moves, but I couldn't find a convincing win, and when I was down to five or six minutes I realized that he didn't have a threat, and that in some lines with my king on b7 there would be some unpleasant checks.
I didn't like 30...♖c8 31.♖c2.
And after 30...♖h4 I was kind of worried to give White two passers, but this should probably be winning somehow: 31.♘xg7 ♖xe4 32.h4 ♖xh4 33.f6 ♖d7.

**31.♖c2**
Neither captures on g7 would work for White: 31.♘xg7 ♘c5 32.♖e1 ♖g8 33.f6 ♖f7 34.♖g6 d3 35.h4 d2 36.♖d1 ♘xe4, and Black wins. And after 31.♖xg7 ♖xg7 32.♘xg7 ♘c5 he cannot keep all his pawns safe.
**31...♖h4 32.♖c4 ♖xe4**

**33.♖xa4**
Giving up the a4-pawn would have been bad if I hadn't spotted a nice idea.
**33...♘c5**
If I remove the e6-knight, then I should easily be winning the pawn

race, with my central pawns against his weaker a- and b-pawns.

**34.♖b4+ ♔c6 35.♖c1 ♖e2!**

A very pleasing idea to play, since I am using my pawns as a shield for my king to run into enemy territory. 35...♔d5 was my initial idea, but I realized that after 36.♖b5 ♖e2 37.b4 is a bit of a problem. ☺

## 'It was even more special because my first trainer witnessed me beating a legend!'

**36...♔d5 37.♖b5 ♔e4 38.♘xc5+ dxc5 39.♖cxc5 d3 40.♔c1 ♔f3**

White resigned. I wasn't expecting resignation just yet, but this should be quite easy to convert.

This win helped my team beat Spain (which I like to call my second home!) 2½-1½. Individually, with this win I was on 5/5. I felt very good, since I had played a very good game and I really felt my flow in the tournament after this win. It was even more special because my first trainer, V. Bhaskar, who was an arbiter in this event, was working on his desk right next to my board and witnessed me beating a legend!

**36.h4** 36.♖bc4 runs into 36...♔d5 37.♘xc5 dxc5 38.♖xc5+ ♔e4.
And luckily 36.♖xd4 won't work: 36...exd4 37.♘xd4+ ♔d5 38.♘xe2 ♖xe2, and White is lost.

Having reached the time-control, things should be quite easy, as my pawns are far more advanced than his.

**41.♖c3 e4 42.♖d5 ♔e3 43.b4 ♖e1+ 44.♔b2 ♔e2**

**NOTES BY**
**Gukesh D**

**Gukesh D**
**Gabriel Sargissian**
Chennai Olympiad 2022 (6)
Queen's Gambit Declined, Ragozin Variation

This game was played in an important match between the two leaders at that point, India 2 and Armenia. I felt good after my win against Shirov the day before, and the next day would be a rest day, so I was motivated to win this game.

**1.d4 d5 2.c4 e6 3.♘f3 ♘f6 4.♘c3**
I play my usual set-up with White, and now the Ragozin was one of the two options I considered likely.

**4...♗b4**
I was happy to see the Ragozin, as I had an interesting idea prepared.

**5.♕a4+ ♘c6 6.e3 0-0 7.♗d2**
Obviously, there are a lot of possible lines to play against the Ragozin. This has been a trendy one.

**7...dxc4 8.♗xc4 ♗d6 9.♕c2 e5 10.dxe5 ♘xe5**

When I prepared for this game I was mostly expecting this position.

**11.♗e2!?**
This idea my trainer GM Vishnu Prasanna found a couple of months back. It's almost a novelty. I had had a couple of chances to use this idea in rapid and blitz games, but I saved it for classical, and I was happy to use it in an important game. The point of this move is just to keep the tension and give Black options.

**11...♘xf3+**
Played after a long think. I didn't think that my opponent would go for this, because when your opponent is in prep (which I'm sure he knew), you try to avoid putting your king in danger.
Instead, 11...♕e7 is the natural way to play.

**12.gxf3** This is the point, of course.

**12...a6**

Black tries to create play on the queenside, since it is now quite clear where my king is going.

**13.0-0-0**
I was not sure if there was a difference between this and the immediate ♖g1.

**13...b5 14.♖hg1 b4**

An interesting move, which prevents ♗c3 after ♘e4.

**15.♘e4 ♘xe4**

**16.fxe4** I thought I was already doing quite well, as I'm leading in

The Indian Dream Team, ready to battle anyone: Praggnanandhaa, 'veteran' Adhiban, Gukesh and Nihal Sarin (Board 5 Raunak Sadwani is missing in the photo).

development and I'm getting f4, and it looks like a very menacing centre. But my dark-squared bishop's lack of elbow room makes the position playable for Black.

After 16.♕xe4 ♖b8 I would love to have the move ♗c3. Here 17.♖xg7+ doesn't work, unfortunately (and 17.♗d3 is met by 17...g6): after 17...♔xg7 18.♖g1+ ♔h8 19.♗d3 f5 Black has repelled the attack.

**16...♕e7 17.f4**

**17...a5?** I thought that 17...f6 was the automatic reply, as I couldn't imagine Black being fine after what happened in the game. Now I was planning to play 18.♖g3, but the comp holds Black's position together: 18...♔h8 19.♖dg1 g6 20.h4, with unclear play. The more direct option was 18.e5 fxe5 19.♗d3 exf4 20.♗xh7+ ♔h8 21.exf4 ♗xf4 22.♗xf4 ♖xf4.

ANALYSIS DIAGRAM

I wasn't sure about this position during the game, but of course the comp says... you guessed it! The famous 0.00...

**18.e5 ♗c5 19.♖g5** I spent quite some time here, and when I saw this move, I got tempted by all the

# 'I wasn't sure about this position but of course the comp says... you guessed it! The famous 0.00...'

geometry with ♖ag1 and f5, when Black cannot take on e5 because of fxg6 and in some lines I was getting e6 to attack the bishop on c5.

There were alternatives to the text-move, and actually the strongest continuation was 19.♕e4!, when both after 19...♗a6 20.f5 and 19...♖b8 20.f5 ♗b7 21.♕f4 White's attack is very dangerous.

**19...♗a6** After I had played 19.♖g5, I realized that 19...g6 is probably good for Black: 20.e6 (20.h4 a4) 20...f5! 21.♗c4, and Black defends.

On the other hand, I thought that my chances should be good after 19...♗b6 20.♖dg1 g6 21.f5 ♕c5 22.♕xc5 ♗xc5 23.e6 ♗e7 24.♖h5.

**20.♖dg1 g6 21.♗xa6 ♖xa6 22.f5**

I felt this position should already be at least close to winning, but there is one, and only one, way for Black to hold.

**22...♖a7?** At first 22...♖c6! did not make sense to me, as I thought there is no threat, but after 23.♔b1 ♖d8 24.e6

fxe6 25.fxg6, 25...h6 is magically holding for Black. But it's very hard to believe in 26.♖5g2 ♕f6.

**23.e6?!** This is inaccurate.

I had seen 23.♔b1!, and I knew it should be winning, but I didn't want to be challenged by stuff like 23...♗c5 24.♕e4 ♖d8, when actually 25.e6 decides the game in White's favour.

**23...♔h8?** Naturally, my opponent did not believe in ...fxe6 either. But he should have: 23...fxe6! 24.fxg6 h6 25.g7 hxg5 26.gxf8♕+ ♔xf8

ANALYSIS DIAGRAM

I had foreseen this position, but as so often I didn't go further and I just thought this should be winning, with the rook and the bishop on the a-file and the king so dangerously placed. But apparently it's not: 27.♕g6 (27.h4 ♕d7) 27...♖c6+ 28.♔b1 ♕f7 29.♕xg5 ♔e8, and Black holds.

Hopeless alternatives were 23...♕c5 24.♕xc5 ♗xc5 25.fxg6 and 23...f6 24.♖5g4 g5 25.h4, which in both cases win easily for White.

**24.♔b1!**

Now it's completely winning. One of the ideas I saw was ♗c1, b3 and ♗b2!!, which just goes to show how dominating my position is.

**24...gxf5**

Allowing me to play a simple but nice trick.

But Black is also lost after 24... f6 25.♖5g4 gxf5 26.♕xf5 ♖xe6 (26...♖xe6 27.♕xh7+ ♔xh7 28.♖h4 mate ☺) 27.♖g7.

**25.♗xb4!**

Now Black has to give up his queen, and there's no hope for a fortress.

**25...♕xb4**

Taking with the pawn also loses: 25...axb4 26.♕g2 ♕d8 27.e7

♕d3+ 28.♔c2 (and not 28.♔a1?? ♖xa2+ 29.♔xa2 b3+ 30.♔a1 ♕a6+ 31.♔b1 ♕d3+ 32.♔a1 ♕a6+ with a perpetual) 28...♕xc2+ 29.♔xc2 ♖e8 30.♖g8+ ♖xg8 31.♖xg8+ ♔xg8 32.e8♕+ ♔g7 33.♕e5+, winning.

**26.♕g2**

**26...♕e4+**

26...♕b8 loses to 27.exf7 ♖g6 28.♖xg6.

**27.♕xe4 fxe4 28.e7 ♖e8 29.♖g8+ ♖xg8 30.♖xg8+ ♔xg8 31.e8♕+ ♔g7**

**32.♕e5+** After I had played this, I saw that there was a quicker win, but OK, it's easy anyway.

Quicker was 32.♕a8 a4 33.♕b7 ♖a5 34.♕xc7 ♖a6 35.♕b7 ♖a5 36.♕xe4 and Black can resign.

**32...♖f6 33.♕g5+ ♖g6 34.♕xa5**

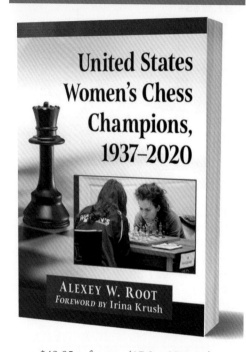
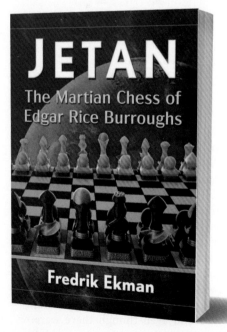

**34...♖g1+**

Of course, Black should avoid 34...♗xe3, because of 35.♕c3+.

**35.♔c2 ♖g2+ 36.♔b3 ♗b6
37.♕e5+**

**37...♔f8**

Also losing is 37...♔g8 38.♕xe4 ♖xh2 39.♕e8+ ♔g7 40.♕e5+ and the rooks drops off.

**38.♕h8+ ♔e7 39.♕xh7 ♖e2**

No better is 39...♖g6, because of 40.♕h4+ and White wins.

**40.♕xe4+ ♔f8 41.♕b4+**

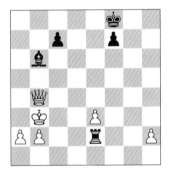

And he loses the rook, so he resigned. Unfortunately, my team lost the match 1½-2½ despite my win.

Full credit to Armenia, who showed great team spirit and played great chess throughout the event and won silver deservedly! And of course Uzbekistan was brilliant and won gold.

I was again very happy with my game. I showed an interesting opening idea and even though there were some inaccuracies from both sides, I was able to navigate the complications better. And 6/6 going into the rest day the tournament looked very promising.

NOTES BY
**Nihal Sarin**

**Sarin Nihal
Sebastian Bogner
Chennai Olympiad 2022 (3)**
Catalan Opening

In Round 3 of the Olympiad we were playing against Switzerland. I had the white pieces against GM Sebastian Bogner, who is usually around 2600 but has lost some rating recently. An interesting fight was ahead!

**1.d4 ♘f6 2.c4 e6 3.♘f3 d5 4.g3 ♗e7 5.♗g2 0-0 6.♕d3!?**

A really new move (first played in 2019!), which was popularized by Catalan experts Boris Gelfand and Jeffery Xiong. It was also tried by Alireza Firouzja against Fabiano Caruana in the Candidates, which surely proves that this move is worth a try.

This looks very similar to the popular 6.♕c2 line, but there are some subtle differences.

**6...♘bd7**

Not the cleanest, but surely playable.

**7.0-0** 7.♘c3!? was also possible, kind of forcing Black to play ...c6 and transpose to a Closed Catalan

**7...b6** I feel that this gives White a very pleasant position. 7...c6 was probably better, going for Closed Catalan set-ups.

**8.cxd5 exd5**

Now I was really happy. This is simply a more pleasant position for White, especially because the bishop is not on b2, as in some Queen's Indian Defence positions.

8...♘xd5 9.a3 looks nice for White.

**9.♘c3 ♗b7 10.♗f4 ♘h5!?**

Giving me a choice.

**11.♖ad1!?**

Objectively not a good move, but the plan to give up the bishop and open the g-file seemed very interesting to me, and it worked out brilliantly in the game. Nevertheless, I would have lost all the advantage if Black had played correctly.

11.e3! is a strong move, according to the engine. I did see this idea, but I was worried about 11...g5, but then 12.g4! would give White a slight advantage.

11.♗d2 ♘hf6 12.♖ac1 is surely also playable.

**11...♘xf4!** Having played the knight to h5 doesn't make sense otherwise.

**12.gxf4 ♖e8 13.♘e5**

**13...♘f6!**

Not a hard move to find, but avoiding the trap 13...♘f8, which seems natural to kick the knight with ...f6, but after 14.♕b5! a6 15.♕b3 c6 16.e4! Black's centre collapses.

**14.e3 c6**

Stopping any ♘b5 or ♕b5 ideas. Around this point, I was beginning to realize that my position looked more attractive than it was, and Black has some easy moves like ...♗d6, ...♕e7, ...♖ad8, ...c5, ...g6, etc. I had to come up with an idea to disrupt this, and fortunately I succeeded.

**15.♔h1!**

Preparing to bring the rooks to the g-file; but it also has a nasty prophylactic idea!

**15...♗d6**

**16.♗f3**

16.♖g1?? ♗xe5! would be a disaster for White.

**16...c5?**

This pawn push looks extremely natural, but it's pretty much the decisive mistake! Black's d5-pawn becomes too weak.

**17.♖g1**

After 17.dxc5, 17...♗xe5 is the point:

Always ready to crack a joke, but dead serious at the board. Nihal Sarin contributed heavily to his team's success with a 2774 performance.

18.fxe5 ♖xe5, and this is okay for Black.

**17...♕e7?!** Played fairly quickly, totally missing my idea.

17...cxd4 would have been a better try: 18.♕xd4 ♗xe5! 19.fxe5 ♘e4. This was worrying me a bit, and I wasn't entirely sure what to do here. I would probably have gone for 20.♗xe4 (20.♘xe4 dxe4 21.♗xe4 ♕xd4 22.♖xd4 ♗xe4+ 23.♖xe4 ♖ac8 looks tenable for Black) 20...dxe4 21.e6! ♕xd4 22.exf7+ ♔xf7 23.♖xd4 ♖ad8 24.♖gd1 ♖xd4 25.♖xd4, and I thought I might be having a slight edge, which the engine confirms.

**18.♘g4!**

At first sight it might seem a bit strange to trade the strong e5-knight, but on closer inspection it is clear that Black just cannot defend his d5-pawn.

**18...♘xg4**

Played after an 18-minute think.

**19.♖xg4 ♖ad8!**

Black finds an excellent defence. It is no longer easy for me to take the d5-pawn and return safely.

**20.♖dg1!**

I was pretty sure this had to be played, but I spent 17 minutes on this move and 11 on the next one, so I was starting to get quite confused. Fortunately, I did manage to come up with good moves.

**20...g6**

**21.♗xd5!**

21.♘xd5 ♕e6 22.f5 looks crushing, but Black has a strong idea: 22...♗xd5!! 23.fxe6 ♗xf3+ 24.♖4g2 ♖xe6, and it's not so clear anymore.

For a long time, I was seriously tempted by 21.f5?!. White just wants to go for the kill at once: 21...♔h8 22.fxg6? fxg6 23.♖xg6.

ANALYSIS DIAGRAM

This seemed to work beautifully, but I realized in time that Black does not need to take the rook here (23...hxg6? 24.♕xg6 ♖f8 25.♖g5!, and White wins), but goes 23...♕f7 and I am lost.

**21...♗xd5+ 22.♘xd5 ♕e6 23.♖g5!**

Now we see the point of including ♖dg1/ ...g6; the rook on g5 is safe now. 23.e4 f5 is no good.

**23...cxd4** After 23...♗f8 24.♖e5 ♕c6 25.♖xe8 (I briefly considered 25.♕e4, but this throws away all the advantage after 25...♖xe5! 26.♘e7+ ♖xe7 27.♕xc6 cxd4) 25...♖xe8 26.dxc5 Black is lost.

**24.e4!** White has stabilized the situation in the centre and can start attacking now.

**24...f5**

**25.f3!** Fairly obvious, but I was so close to blundering with 25.♕xd4?? ♗c5! (25...♗f8!? is what I was worried about, and this is good enough for equality: 26.♕f6 ♕xe4+. I did see the check here! Can't explain!) 26.♕f6?? ♕xe4+, and for some reason I missed that this was a check.

**25...♖f8?**

The final mistake. Too much pressure on the board and the clock.

He should have tried 25...fxe4 26.fxe4, but the position remains really bad for Black.

**26.exf5!** The only way for an advantage, but this wins immediately.

**26...♕xd5 27.fxg6**

Next there will be gxh7+ and ♕xd4, and Black either gets mated or loses a lot of material, so he resigned.

NOTES BY
## Adhiban Baskaran

**Adhiban Baskaran
Eduardo Iturrizaga
Chennai Olympiad 2022 (5)**
Nimzo-Indian Defence, Sämisch Variation

Welcome to Chennai! I was very proud to be part of this Olympiad, since it was organized in my home town of Chennai. Additionally, this time was such a fun experience because I was part of the young vibrant team (excluding myself of course ☺) India 2, comprising of Gukesh, Nihal, Pragg, and Raunak. It made for a welcome change after my previous editions!

This particular match was very special for me, since I felt I played a great game and won a crucial victory, helping our team to defeat Spain.

For this event, I stuck to the Queen's Pawn Opening.

**1.d4 ♘f6 2.c4 e6**

My opponent's usual preference is the solid Nimzo/Queen's-Indian.

**3.♘c3 ♗b4 4.e3 0-0 5.a3!?**

I was aiming for a complex battle, and this seemed like a good approach.

**5...♗xc3+ 6.bxc3 c5 7.♗d3 d5**

I couldn't believe my eyes when he played this! My opponent had already played this move before, in 2019, and I had never expected that he would do it again!

**8.cxd5 ♕xd5** Taking back with the e-pawn is preferable.

**9.♘f3**

9.f3, followed by ♘e2, was very tempting, but I felt it was unnecessary.

**9...b6**

This is Black's main concept, trying to fight for the light squares and the potential hanging pawns structure.

**10.c4**

10.♕e2 was the correct execution of the plan I was aiming for, with a nice pawn centre and the bishop pair advantage after 10...♗b7 11.e4. The e4-pawn is untouchable: after 11...♘xe4? 12.c4 Black will lose the piece due to the pin or ♘e5, over-loading the queen.

**10...♕c6**

For 10...♕h5 I had planned 11.g4! ♕xg4 (11...♘xg4 12.♗e4 wins material due to Black's poor development) 12.♖g1 ♕h5 13.♖g5, with a very powerful initiative due to the open g-file and the mighty bishop pair.

**11.♕e2**

I tried to punish his concept by preparing e4, which wasn't needed. Natural and very good was 11.0-0 ♗b7 12.♗b2 ♘bd7 13.a4, leading to a sound advantage thanks to the bishop pair.

**11...♗b7**

Don't mess with Adhiban! 'I felt I played a great game and won a crucial victory, helping our team to defeat Spain.'

**12.0-0**

After burning quite some time I told myself that e4 was not going to work today ☺: 12.e4 cxd4 13.e5 ♘fd7 14.♗xh7+ ♔xh7 15.♘g5+ ♔g6! (Braveheart!) 16.♕d3+ f5! (I had completely missed this defensive resource) 17.exf6+ ♔xf6, and the king runs to the centre and from there might go to the queenside, leaving me with less material and without any attacking chances.

**12...♘bd7 13.♗b2**

First finishing development. 13.a4!? was also very good.

**13...♖fd8 14.a4!**

Time to extend my power!

**14...♖ac8 15.a5**

I felt that if I got rid of my a-pawn... I would have the ultimate pawn structure!

15.♖fd1 is the comp's preference, with quite a large advantage. I have noticed that the engine gives a lot of practical value to the bishop pair.

## 'I have noticed that the engine gives a lot of practical value to the bishop pair'

**15...♕c7 16.axb6 axb6**

The drawback of my plan was that Black now uses the a-file to exchange the rooks, reducing my winning potential.

**17.♘d2!**

Preventing ♗e4 and maintaining the bishop pair.

**17...♖a8 18.♖fd1**

I decided to give him the move, as I wasn't sure if h3 was needed right now.

**18...♖xa1 19.♖xa1 ♖a8 20.♖xa8+**

It didn't look as if a fight for the a-file was necessary... So I decided to focus on the central affairs.

**20...♗xa8**

**21.h3**

Freeing the queen by avoiding any future ...♘g4 jumps.

21.f3 might have been better, and it was my first instinct, but didn't feel like weakening the kingside squares. But at the same time he doesn't have the necessary dark-squared bishop to make use of it ☺!

**21...h6 22.♕e1!?**

Her majesty is getting ready to oversee her subjects to the final war ☺.

**22...♗c6 23.♗f1**

Now I have protected my only weak point, which was the g2-pawn.

**23...cxd4** I was happy to see this, as it wasn't necessary to relax the central pressure! Now I will have the required free hand to go into Phase 2!

23...♕a7 was Black's best bet, leading to a defendable endgame.

**24.exd4 ♕b7**

Preparing ...b5.

**25.♘b3** Tactically preventing it, by threatening ♘a5.

**25...♕a8 26.♕b4**

The queen occupies a commanding position, while ...♕a2 can be met by ♘c1.

**26...♗e4**

Around here, my opponent started losing track, since there were no active plans available. For instance, 26...♕a2 27.♘c1 ♕b1 28.♗d3, and suddenly Black's queen is trapped.

**27.♘d2** Kicking the bishop back.

**27...♗c6 28.♘b1!**

Since the position was fully under control, it was time to improve my pieces. I felt that my knight was the only piece that could be improved... I decided to bring it to e3.

**28...♗e4 29.♘c3 ♗c6 30.♘d1!**

On c3, the knight gets in the way of our beautiful Nimzo-Larsen bishop ☺.

**30...♕b8 31.♘e3** Very happy to bring the knight to e3.

**31...♕f4 32.♕e1**

Just protecting my king and making it feel at ease with its queen having everything under control.

**32...♗b7**

**33.d5!** Time to cash in! I felt that all my pieces were optimally placed and that it was time to do something.

**33...exd5** 33...♘c5, trying to maintain the tension, wouldn't work due to 34.g3, and the queen can't maintain control over f6 and the b6-pawn, which can be targeted with ♕b4.

**34.cxd5**

# 'One of the biggest advantages of a bishop over a knight is that... we can often choose the moment to exchange it!'

The d-pawn is untouchable due to a tactical point.

**34...♕e4**

One sample line would be 34...♘xd5 35.♘xd5 ♗xd5 36.♕e8+ ♘f8 37.♗a3, winning the f8-knight.

After 34...♗xd5 there would follow 35.♘xd5 ♘xd5 36.♕e8+ ♘f8 37.♗a3 ♘b4 38.♕e7, and Black loses one of his knights.

**35.f3** I felt the queen was too good on e4, and I wanted to kick it.

**35...♕f4 36.♕c3**

Keeping pressure along the diagonal and continuing to prevent Black's capture of the d5-pawn.

**36...♘c5 37.♗b5!** Preventing ...♘a4 and preparing ♗c6 ideas.

**37...♕g5** 37...♔h8 was the move I felt was best. Not yet defining the location of the pieces.

**38.♗c6 ♗xc6** My opponent collapsed in time-trouble, but 38...♗c8 39.♕e5 looked crushing.

**39.dxc6 ♘e6 40.♕e5!**

After the queen swap the advanced c-pawn would probably win one of the knights.

**40...♘c7 41.♕xc7**

This looked the cleanest.

**41...♕xe3+ 42.♔h2 ♕e8 43.♕d6!**

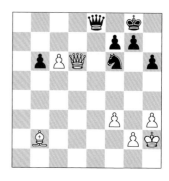

One of the biggest advantages of a bishop over a knight is that... we can often choose the moment to exchange it!

**43...♕c8 44.♗xf6 gxf6 45.♕d7**

Black resigned.

An important win, which helped us win the match against Spain, as Gukesh won an epic game against Shirov, and Nihal drew.

This moved India 2 to second place on the leader board of the Olympiad. I was quite happy with my play, since most of my moves were the engine's top choices!

NOTES BY
**Anish Giri**

**Anish Giri**
**Baadur Jobava**
Chennai Olympiad 2022 (6)
King's Indian Defence

**1.d4 ♘f6 2.c4 c5 3.d5 g6 4.♘c3 ♗g7 5.e4 d6 6.♘f3 0-0 7.♗e2 e6 8.0-0 exd5 9.exd5**

This old variation is supposed to be better for White. In fact, nowadays it is often played with a tempo less for White, via the 1.d4 ♘f6 2.c4 g6 3.♘f3 ♗g7 4.e3 0-0 5.♗e2 variation of the Grünfeld. White later plays e3-e4, with the loss of an entire tempo, and still tries to fight for an advantage.

**9...♗g4** Black is short of space, so trading the bishop is sensible.
**10.h3 ♗xf3 11.♗xf3 ♘bd7 12.♗f4?!**

I am not sure if my play at this stage of the game was ideal. Black wants ...♘e8 anyway, which I realized later, so I am not sure there is a point to this move at all.
**12...♘e8 13.♕d2 ♘e5 14.♗e2 f5 15.♖fe1 ♘f7**

15....♗f6, intending ...g5, was also interesting.
**16.♖ab1**

I wanted to keep b4 ideas, and later, if Black trades with ...cxb4, I had some

## 'Little did I know that in this game the e6-square was reserved for the rook'

♘b5-d4-e6 hopes. Little did I know that in this game the e6-square was reserved for the rook.
**16...g5!** A good idea to expand, but when Black played it, I felt it was premature.
**17.♗h2**

**17...♗e5?!** 17...f4! was actually good. I felt I should be able to use all the light squares, but it seems that shutting off the h2-bishop is worth it for Black.
**18.♗h5** The most practical option.
**18...♗xh2+?!** Human, but the engine prefers to still play 18...f4, or even 18...♗xc3!? first. **19.♔xh2**

**19...♘g7?**
This was very surprising, as Black clearly must have intended to play ...♘e5 here. With nothing blocking the e-file now, White's plan is quite obvious.

We had some disagreement about the position arising after 19...♘e5!, with my opponent being optimistic about his chances. In fact, it seems my intuition was correct, in that there is an issue with Black's position here as well: 20.♗xe8! ♖xe8 21.f4! gxf4 22.♕xf4

**ANALYSIS DIAGRAM**

and here Black has to go for the sad 22...♖f8, when after the ♖e3-g3, ♖f1, ♘e2 regrouping White has a large advantage. But we both assumed that the natural 22...♕f6 was the point. Now, however, there is a simple sequence: 23.♘e4! ♕g6 24.♘xc5!. I think I even saw this far, but I wasn't sure what was going on after 24...♖ac8. I can try to be greedy with 25.b4 b6 26.♖e3, which is probably the direction in which I would have been thinking, but the engine points out a very elegant and clean solution: 25.♘e6! ♖xc4 26.♘d4!.

Anish Giri had the fifth best result on Board 1. The Dutchman's fine win against Baadur Jobava provided a textbook example of an exchange sacrifice.

was also very much into 25.♕f4!?). 25...♕xh3+ 26.♔g1 ♔h8 27.e7 ♖e8 28.♕f4 ♖g6 29.♕xf5, and it's lights out.

**25.♕f4** As I mentioned earlier, there are many wins at this point.

**25...gxh3 26.g3 ♖c8**

**27.♕xf5** I just went for the win in the endgame. 27.e7 ♕d7 28.g4!? wins in the middle game.

**27...♕f8 28.♕xf8+**

Once again, the simplest approach.

## 'In this case I have the perfect version, with each remaining piece having a clear purpose'

**28...♔xf8 29.f4 ♖e8 30.f5 ♖g5 31.♖f1 ♖g4 32.♖f4**

The most stylish way, although literally any other reasonable idea would have been winning. Shutting the window for the last piece that tried to be active. After 32...♖xf4 33.gxf4 Black can't move at all.

Black resigned. ∎

**ANALYSIS DIAGRAM**

Let's take a moment and appreciate this regrouping. White is positionally winning now, with the f5-pawn doomed.

**20.♗xf7+ ♖xf7 21.♖e6!**

It didn't take too long to spot this,

and as soon as I did, I knew this was a good move. This sacrifice in this structure feels thematic, but in this particular case, more than ever, I have the perfect version, with each remaining piece having a clear purpose (the knight heading to d5, etc.) and no superfluous pieces.

**21...♘xe6 22.dxe6 ♖g7 23.♘d5**

The position is playing itself. The rest of the game is essentially converting, and often my moves were just a matter of taste, with plenty of alternative winning continuations.

**23...g4 24.♖e1**

Everything is in the game.

**24...♖g6** After 24...♕h4, 25.g3! would be the roughest (although I

# Dommaraju Gukesh:

# 'It's kind of sad for the entire world if Magnus doesn't defend his title'

The absolute headliner of the Chennai Olympiad was 16-year-old Gukesh, the leader of the host's 'junior team', India 2. His stunning run of eight consecutive wins was one for the ages, and his gold medal on Board 1 provided further proof of his incredible potential. In an interview with **DIRK JAN TEN GEUZENDAM**, the Indian star speaks freely about his self-confidence, his ambitions and his role model, 'Anand sir'. And while doing so, he extends a big thank-you to Gata Kamsky.

**W**hen you talk to Gukesh, you are naturally drawn into the calm and composure that he exudes. You cannot but observe him, as he quietly but firmly voices his thoughts. Self-assured without a trace of arrogance; humble in way, but not making a humble impression at all. Once a shy child prodigy who replied to journalists in monosyllables and even sign language, he now feels at ease expressing his thoughts and fluidly answers questions, rarely chewing on one. With the beard that he is sporting these days and his bright confident eyes, he looks like a dashing young film star, and you

have to remind yourself that he is only 16 years old.

Three years ago, Gukesh appeared on the cover of New In Chess – a young boy in the back garden of his family's home in Korattur, a quiet area on the outskirts of Chennai. Underneath the photo was the question: Will he be the next Indian World Champion? Inside the magazine, Gukesh, at that time the second-youngest GM in history, was presented to the reader in an engrossing profile penned by V. Saravanan. The Indian chess journalist visited the 13-year-old super talent at his home and spoke to his parents, his father Dr. Dommaraju Rasjni-

kanth, a nose and throat surgeon, and his mother Dr. Padma Kumari, a microbiologist. He also spoke to Gukesh's trainer, GM Vishnu Prasanna, who was quoted memorably as saying: 'The kid is running at a very fast pace! (...) I think he can go all the way, to the very top. But I don't want him to chase things. You have to be interested in chess. There should be passion for the game, a desire to understand its mystery. And you succeed once you do.'

Three years on, Gukesh's understanding of the mystery of chess has grown enormously. His recent results, capped by a breath-taking run of

'Personally, I am very good at handling pressure recently. I think pressure makes me perform at my best.'

eight wins and a gold medal on Board 1 at the Chennai Olympiad, have only strengthened the idea that he might very well be the next Indian World Champion. Under his leadership, the young team of India 2 finished third and had good reason to think that they had missed out on winning the Olympiad. Individually, Gukesh is closing in on the world's top-20, and he keeps rising. His games are profound and bedazzling. And, as said, as he answered our questions after the Olympiad, he did so with the class, introspection and dignity of a champion.

*Right from the start, there was a lot of sympathy for India 2. Many people were rooting for 'the youngsters' and hoping you'd do better than India 1. How did that feel?*
'It was not a big surprise, because the four of us, me, Pragg (17), Nihal (18) and Raulak (16) are youngsters and we can perform at the highest level on our best days. And Adhiban (29) is very experienced, he is also a very strong player on his best days. It felt good to see so much support, and I think we were up to the task.'

*It must also have come with pressure; besides, you were playing in your home city. How did you deal with that?*
'Personally, I am very good at handling pressure recently. I think pressure makes me perform at my best. It was just nice to see so much support. It motivated me to do well and I think it was the same for the whole team.'

*Many people would love to know how to handle pressure. Is it some sort of a mental trick? How do you do that?*
'(Smiling) For some people it's natural to block all negative things. They can use it to their advantage. But for me it's more extreme discipline and training. In the pandemic I spent quite a lot of time with my coach Vishnu sir [adding 'sir' – or 'mam',

short for madam, in case of a woman – is an Indian way of showing respect, for instance for a teacher or coach – DJtG] trying to find the ideal mental state of handling pressure. I think it is very well possible to turn pressure and expectations into a positive thing. Just push yourself with that pressure to perform at your best. During the past few months, this was one of the main reasons for my very good performances. I've been doing a lot of things, one of which is meditation. That has really helped me, and I practise it regularly.'

# 'I meditate for 10 to 15 minutes, usually before the game'

*It helps you to become calm and focused...*
'Not necessarily... You can also get a bit like excited. The thing is, you can be emotional, but you should not allow that to influence your game. This is why people say that emotion is not good. But if you are able to prevent those emotions from influencing your decisions or your moves – that's a very good thing.'

*You let them be there, but they are not going to influence your thinking process.*
'For example, I think that nervousness is a very positive thing, because it gives you the extra thing that makes you perform, to achieve something special. As long as you do not try to fight it. Just let the nervousness be there, and you just do your work. Nervousness is good for you, as long as you don't fight it.'

*You say that an essential part of your mental training has been meditation. How does that work in a tournament? What do you do?*
'During a tournament I follow the regular things that I also do at home.

I meditate for 10 to 15 minutes, usually before the game. And after the game it's usually something physical, like a walk.'

*Meditation before the game, is that trying to empty your head? How would you explain that to someone who doesn't know what meditation is?*
'There are a lot of variations in meditation, and one of the things I mostly do is follow my breathing. I don't know, it just takes you away from the game a bit. Just to not get any thoughts before the game.'

*Fully concentrating on your breathing?*
'Yeah, just understanding yourself.'

*What does that mean, understanding yourself?*
'When you just follow your breath, you know what thoughts are there, what kind of thoughts you are getting. You try to block them, fully focusing on your breathing.'

*You knew all the people on the team very well. But now suddenly you were a team. How did you create a team spirit?*
'I think it just came automatically. All of us are very, very good friends. We've known each other for a very long time. There were a lot of jokes at our team meetings and we were laughing a lot. I mean, when we needed to be serious, we were serious. Nihal probably has the best sense of humour. And Pragg is the bad jokes guy. And Adhiban is the talkative one.'

*Is it typical Indian humour or what kind of humour is it?*
'In this team, me, Pragg and Adhiban, we are from the same state. As you know, in India there are so many languages. So for us it's usually some Tamil-related jokes. I'm not sure I can call it Indian humour... Probably more generational.'

*You have your own coach, Vishnu Prasanna, but now the head coach of* the team was Ramesh. What kind of experience was that? What did he ask you to focus on?

'When it came to preparation I didn't spend much time with other team mates or the coaches or seconds. The others had a couple of training camps before the Olympiad, which I was not a part of, because I was playing some tournaments and I was also a bit sick at some point. Even during the Olympiad, I mainly worked with my own coach, and the others were working amongst themselves. When it came to the chess part, I think this came mainly down to the seconds, (GMs) Stany and Arjun Kalyan. They did the most important chess parts and Ramesh was, I am not sure, he was thinking about the board order and some general advice and stuff.

'In the months leading up to the Olympiad, I had a four-week training session with my coach, during which we worked a lot. During the Olympiad he came to visit me, and he was following the games, but we did not talk about openings and stuff. It had all been done already beforehand.'

*This was a team competition, but of course you have your own interests, too. Were you ready to share opening information?*

'(Slightly surprised) Eh, between the team members? I honestly am not sure what the others were doing, but for me... OK, if it's some general thing like in the Sicilian, this move order is better than this move order, and such subtleties, I was fine with sharing, but opening ideas I am definitely not comfortable with sharing with the group.'

*Things went extremely well and you scored one full point after the other, going from three to four, five wins... How did you try to keep a cool head?*

'Actually, I should specially thank Gata Kamsky for this event. Not because I have worked with him or anything, but in Biel I had a great learning experience. I was playing in

the tournament with him and during the closing ceremony I was talking to him. And then he said that during the first classical games I played like myself, and I scored two and a half out of three, and I was leading the tournament halfway through the event. Then I tried to change my style and be solid and maintain my position. Kamsky told me, you should play like yourself no matter what the tournament standings are. You should just try to win, because that's who you are. He said that being solid does not necessarily mean that you will protect your tournament situation. Because in Biel, after I tried to be solid, I lost a couple of games, and Le Quang Liem overtook me.

'That was something that Kamsky made me realize, and it really helped at the Olympiad. I got three wins, and then kept playing for a win, four, five, six, seven. Even after the eighth win against Fabi (Fabiano Caruana)... Before the event I thought that eight out of eleven would be a very good score. And suddenly I was on 8 out of 8 and I thought, what just happened? (Smiles) But even after the Fabi win I remembered Kamsky's advice and I did not try to change my style and I was going for the win in every game. OK, I can't say that this really

## 'Kamsky told me, you should play like yourself no matter what the standings are'

helped, because I over-pressed and lost against Abdusattorov. But I really enjoyed being myself. That is something that Kamsky made me realize.'

*For Gata Kamsky there was no doubt that you are a maximalist and that you should be true to yourself.*

# Dommaraju Gukesh

**Born:** May 29, 2006, Chennai, India

**Career highlights**
2013: Learns to play chess
2015: Gold at U-9 World Schools
2018: Cappelle-la-Grande, final IM norm
5 Gold medals at the Asian Youth Championships
Under-12 World Champion
2019: February FIDE rating: 2508
2019: Delhi, final GM norm
Second youngest GM ever at 12 years, 7 months, 27 days
2021: After a year of non-activity tops Bangladesh League scoring 9½/10
2021: Wins Norway Chess Open
2021: Wins Concello de Carballo Clasico scoring 8 from 9
2021: October FIDE rating: 2640
2022: Wins Chessable Sunway Formentera Festival scoring 8 from 10
2022: Wins Cerrado Ciudad de Gijon scoring 8 from 9
2022: August FIDE rating: 2699
2022: Chennai Olympiad, gold medal Board 1, Performance rating 2867
2022: September FIDE rating: 2726 (24th in the world ranking)

'Yeah. The main thing that I learned in Biel is to not fight myself, to be true to myself. And I think in the Olympiad I was true to myself, and even though I got a heart-breaking loss against Abdusattorov, I am still fine with it.'

*When you got to 7 out of 7, did you think of Caruana's 7 out of 7 in St. Louis in the 2015 Sinquefield Cup?*

'Yes, I remembered it, it was at the back of my mind. I didn't really spend a lot of time thinking about it, but I had a very nice thought that if I beat Fabi and break his record, it will be something I'll be proud of.'

*You got to 8 out of 8, by beating him, of all people. Were you then thinking of Kramnik's 8½ out of 9 at his Olympiad debut, or did that never cross your mind?*

'I knew that when Kramnik played in '92 (at the Manila Olympiad), he scored really well, but I did not know the exact numbers of wins he scored. But when I was on 8 out of 8, I thought that I was probably close to his record or had even already beaten it.'

*Which were the wins that you were most proud of?*

'My game against Sargissian I was really proud of. And also against Shirov. I think I showed no fear in that game. When Shirov played Rook g1 and then pushed g4, it was not a very good idea, but when Shirov plays it, you know you have to watch out. I just looked at the position and I realized that it was not a very good idea. And I calmly refuted it. And in the end, I kind of psychologically tricked him, inviting him to play d4. Yeah, both these games I was quite happy with.'

*Then, as you already mentioned, there came that dark day when you lost from a winning position against Abdusattorov. How did you cope with that?*

'I should thank Vishy sir for this, because after the game I was completely devastated. For about half an hour I was just completely broken, but then Vishy offered to talk with me. He and Aruna mam contacted my father. Vishy was in the same hotel as where we were. He asked if I wanted to speak with him. We spent some one and a half hours, two hours, talking and I can't thank him enough.

'I have been working at the Anand Chess Academy, and this has been a blessing. I learned so many things. He has always been my role model, and being closely in touch with him is something I really couldn't have imagined.

'For a brief time, we kind of discussed my game with Abdusattorov. OK, he said, you should not have lost this position, but it happens sometimes. And then he started showing me his examples from his playing days. When he was pushing for a win and there was nothing special, just having this loss of concentration, completely spoiling winning positions. And obviously everything I am going through he's already been through a hundred times. It was great to get advice and see examples of such a great player.

*You say that Anand is not only an inspiration as a player, but also as a person. Maybe it is a bit unusual to realize at your age how important it is to be a good person as well. Is it something*

# 'I should thank Vishy sir for this. I was completely devastated and then he offered to talk with me'

*your parents have taught you? Is it part of Indian upbringing?*

'It's probably part of Indian upbringing. Especially my mom has always told me: I will be extremely happy when people say Gukesh is a great chess player, but I'll be even happier when they say he is an even better human being. That is something my parents have been very particular about, being polite and humble, no matter how great I am. My parents always told me I should be like Vishy sir.'

*You come across as very calm and in control. Is that your personality, or is there insecurity underneath as well. How confident are you?*

'When it comes to chess I am quite confident. Especially the last few months. I've always been confident, but especially during the last few months I have felt that my confidence has been sky-high. There are different ways to show your confidence, and my way of showing it is just to play good games.'

*You sound so mature and you're only 16 years old. What I was impressed by was that you preferred not to hear the pairings for the next day, because you thought it was more important to sleep well. That might be the result of years of experience, but it's not something that I would automatically expect from a young player. How did you get that idea?*

'It was also partly due to Vishy sir. [After the loss to Abdusattorov] I told him that I didn't feel like looking at chess right now. So should I prepare for tomorrow or just sleep? And he said: You have played games already and for your age, you should not be forgetting things so easily. You'll probably just revise something that you've already seen at least a couple of times in the last weeks. There's no point in torturing yourself. He just advised me to sleep.'

*But it wasn't only before the last round that you thought sleeping well was more important than knowing your opponent.*

'Yeah, during tournaments, when there is an afternoon round, I don't see the pairings before I sleep, because I just want to get some good sleep. In the morning I wake up and see the pairings and I still have time to prepare. I used to see the pairings at night, but then I realized at some point that it's getting in my head while I am sleeping.

'Also during the Olympiad I didn't know any of the board pairings before I went to sleep. But I knew the team we were going to play because we had some team meetings to discuss the board orders.'

*There is a general consensus that this Olympiad we saw a breakthrough of the new generation. Does it feel that way?*

'I don't think I can say so right now.

You can't judge by one tournament, but it really feels like something special. But time will tell. But I think Abdusattorov, I mean, this is not the first time he has broken through, he's the World Rapid Champion (smiles). So...'

*Is it a great feeling to be part of a generation that is clearly so promising?*
'Sure, I don't think there was any generation where there was such a great competition. For instance, from my own country there are four or five others, very super-strong talents. Then there is Abdusattorov, Keymer, I mean, so many other guys. It's a very positive thing, and part of the reason why we are all performing so well. Because we all see someone is winning the World Rapid Championship, someone is winning the Tata Steel Challengers, and someone is winning Olympiad gold, and we all get motivated by that and try to improve on our previous achievements. That is something that really motivates us. We try to be the best amongst ourselves.'

*The age-old dream of the youngsters has always been to be World Champion. You want to play for the World Championship. Now this may be your dream, but if the Champion doesn't defend his title... When Magnus Carlsen said that, did that come as a blow to you? Did it feel as if he was taking away something from you?*
'That's the goal of all the youngsters. I mean, for myself, my goal has always been to be the best in the world, to be World Champion someday. But yeah, it's kind of sad for the entire world if Magnus doesn't defend. I mean, he has already said so, but when he was hinting about that I was hoping that it's not true. But I also know that Magnus usually says what he thinks and when Nepo won, I thought that he most probably wouldn't defend...

'It's kind of sad for the entire world, because Magnus is clearly the best player in the world, and a World

STEV BONHAGE

**Every day, before his opponent arrived, Gukesh first faced an army of photographers.**

Championship without Magnus Carlsen will probably not be the same. It's kind of sad, but I also understand

## 'My goal has always been to be the best in the world, to be World Champion someday'

his position. He's already played five World Championships. I mean, for example, this Olympiad was so stressful for me. I can't imagine what a World Championship feels like.'

*Despite all the meditation and everything, it was very stressful...*
'Sure. I was enjoying the event, but there was always stress. I was always

thinking about my next game. I was completely into the Olympiad, I don't even know how to explain it.'

*Did you gradually feel depleted, feel the energy going?*
'Maybe it happened, but I did not feel it. Maybe I just did not pay attention to it. I was just thinking about the next game all the time.'

*So after the Olympiad you were a relieved and happy person.*
'But also kind of sad. First of all, there was the disappointment of bronze and not gold, I mean, we were very close to gold. But I was also happy that it was a great performance overall, and that the Olympiad was such a great celebration of chess. I was also kind of missing it. Suddenly it was gone. I spent a lot of time with my friends on the last day. With mixed feelings, but also good feelings.' ∎

Team captain Michail Brodsky lifts the trophy for the Ukrainian women: Anna and Mariya Muzychuk, Nataliya Buksa, Yuliia Osmak and Anna Ushenina.

# Glory to Ukraine in Women's Olympiad

## Gold medals bring pride to war-torn country

In a very close race that went down to the wire, Ukraine's women's team sensationally took first place when top-seeds India stumbled in a dramatic final round. Ukraine's victory on the chess board offered a symbolic glimmer of hope for the millions that continue to suffer under the brutal Russian invasion. The team's happiness and pride only grew when Ukrainian president Volodymyr Zelensky sent his congratulations.

As in the Open section, China and Russia were conspicuously absent in the Women's Olympiad for well-known reasons. China continues to struggle with the effects of their Covid restrictions, while Russia was banned for the military invasion of Ukraine.

Without the two strongest countries in women's chess, the top favourites in Chennai seemed to be India (rating average 2486), Ukraine (2478) and Georgia (2475). But how indicative are starting lists if we look at what happened in the Open section, where none of the top-3 seeds reached the podium and none of the top-3 finishers had even featured in the top-10 of the starting list? '

Funnily enough, while the race in the Open section was full of surprises, upsets and statistic anomalies, the Women's Olympiad faithfully followed an almost uncannily predictable scenario, with all three top-seeds ending up on the winners' podium.

For a long time, the highest rated team of India 1, led by Humpy Koneru, seemed to be on course to bring the host country its first ever Olympiad victory. Particularly Board 3, R. Vaishali (Pragg's sister) and Board 4, highly popular Chess24 commentator Tanya Sachdev, were on fire, with the latter ultimately taking the bronze medal on Board 4. After 7 rounds India had won all their matches and were two match points clear of Ukraine, Armenia and Georgia. However, the next rounds showed that the margins were indeed small when India drew with Ukraine and lost to Poland.

Nevertheless, India entered the last round in the lead, one match point ahead of no fewer than four teams: Poland, Azerbaijan, Ukraine and Georgia. The final day was bitter for the local fans, as India lost 1-3 to the United States and had to content themselves with third place. Georgia lashed out against Azerbaijan, 3-1,

securing second place, with Nino Batsiashvili winning another game and securing an individual gold medal on Board 2.

The big winners of the last day were Ukraine, who defeated Poland 3-1 and leapfrogged India to win the Women's Olympiad. The team was led by Mariya Muzychuk, with her sister Anna on Board 2 and Anna Ushenina on Board 3. Both Anna Muzychuk and Anna Ushenina won individual silver medals on

## The big winners of the last day were Ukraine, who defeated Poland 3-1 and leapfrogged India to win the Women's Olympiad

their boards. Ushenina (36) was the 'veteran' on the team, and the only member who had also played on the Ukrainian team that won the Olympiad for the first time in Turin in 2006 (interestingly, ahead of Russia and China!).

The Muzychuk sisters can look back on one of the biggest successes in their rich chess career and a most memorable moment in their country's history. To begin with, Mariya annotates her crucial win from the all-deciding last round.

### NOTES BY
### Mariya Muzychuk

**Mariya Muzychuk**
**Alina Kashlinskaya**
Chennai Olympiad 2022 (11)
French Defence, Winawer Variation

This game was played in the last round, which almost always is the

most important one. Our team knew that if we won the match, we would definitely be in the Top-3. Therefore we were highly motivated. We also knew that if we won, there was a chance we would even become the ultimate winners, but this required additional help from the other teams ☺.

I am very happy that all the stars aligned on that day. It was one of my dreams to win the Olympiad, and I'm glad that my win against Alina Kashlinskaya contributed to the overall success.

**1.e4 e6**
The game was played in the morning and apart from the French I also had to prepare for several other openings. I have played many games against Alina. Our encounters ended in different results, but one thing was constant – Alina was always well-prepared in the opening phase. So I had to be really careful with choosing what I was going to play and repeat various lines meticulously.
**2.d4 d5 3.♘c3 ♗b4 4.e5 ♘e7 5.a3 ♗xc3+ 6.bxc3 c5 7.♕g4 ♕c7**

This line is known to be very sharp. Black 'invites' White to take two pawns, then takes them back and then sacrifices material again ☺. The ensuing positions are very chaotic; the theory has been developed as far as moves 30-40, and one definitely cannot play this variation just relying on making moves based on 'common sense'.
**8.♕xg7** Accepting the challenge. 8.♗d3 is a serious alternative, but

8.♕xg7 is obviously the most principled move.

**8...♖g8 9.♕xh7 cxd4 10.♘e2 ♘bc6 11.f4 dxc3 12.♕d3 d4**

At top level, 12...d4 started to be played in 2009. But many strong grandmasters became a fan of it – many lines are forced and the engines confirm that Black is OK here. On the other hand, the old-fashioned 12...♗d7 is not considered to be credible these days.

On the final day Mariya Muzychuk won a crucial game against Alina Kashlinskaya and then saw all the stars align.

**13.♘xd4 ♘xd4 14.♕xd4 ♗d7 15.♖g1** Many years ago, my sister Anna tried the mirrored move with the other rook. Black also has to know what to do after 15.♖b1, but for this game I had prepared 15.♖g1.

**15...♘f5 16.♕f2 ♕c6 17.♗d3 ♕d5**

**18.♗e3**

18.♖b1 is also a popular move in this position, but with 18.♗e3 I was still following my prep. The idea of ♖b1 is to win the c3-pawn. The game usually continues with 18...♗c6 19.♖b3 0-0-0 20.♖xc3 ♔b8, and although it's already move 20, there are many theoretical continuations that are already well-known. Black

is doing well here. The activity of Black's pieces and White's king in the centre fully compensate the two missing pawns.

**18...♘xe3 19.♕xe3 ♖xg2 20.♖xg2 ♕xg2 21.♗e4 ♕xh2**

And suddenly Black is a pawn up! But White finishes her development with castling and takes the initiative.

**22.0-0-0** Normally you should castle before move 22 ☺. But in this sharp line, which basically starts with 8.♕xg7, White often does not have a chance to castle at all. So, castling and moving the king to a safe place is considered to be a success.

**22...♗c6**

The only move. Unfortunately, Black doesn't have time to do the same: 22...0-0-0 is known to be losing due to 23.♕xc3+ ♔b8 (or 23...♗c6 24.♗xc6 ♕xf4+ 25.♔b2 ♖xd1 26.♗f3+, winning) 24.♕b4 ♕xf4+ 25.♔b1 b6 26.♕d6+ ♔c8 27.♗c6, and White wins.

**23.♗xc6+**

23.♔b1 is another interesting opportunity, which also forces Black to find (or memorize) the precise way to equality: 23...♗xe4! 24.♕xe4 ♕f2! 25.♕xb7 ♕b6+! 26.♕xb6 axb6, and this is equal.

**23...bxc6 24.♕d4**

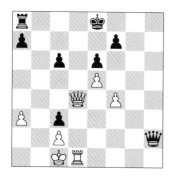

**24...a5**

Played quite quickly, which meant that Alina had this position analyzed at home. But somewhere around here I started feeling that she wasn't so confident, which is an important sign in long theoretical battles.

24...a5 looks a bit mysterious, but its idea will be seen later. In fact, in this position there are only three moves for Black that do not lead to an immediate loss, and 24...a5 is one of them.

24...♕e2!? is a good alternative, when after 25.♕xc3 ♕e4 centralizes the queen and attacks f4. I believe Black should eventually equalize.

24...♕g2 does not lose, but I don't recommend it: 25.♕d7+ ♔f8 26.♔b7 ♖e8 27.♕xa7 ♕f3 28.♕d4, and here Black should have analyzed everything to a draw, or you'd better choose 24...a5 or 24...♕e2.

24...♔f8 has been tried but loses after 25.♔b1! ♖b8 26.♔a1!. White threatens ♖g1, followed by ♕d6+ or ♕c5+, while taking on c2 doesn't work: 26...♕xc2 27.♕d6+ ♔g7 28.♖g1+ ♔h7 29.♕xb8.

**25.f5**

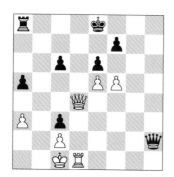

**25...exf5**

25...♕h6+!? 26.♔b1 exf5 was another

# 'Around here I started feeling that she wasn't so confident, which is an important sign in long theoretical battles'

'healthy' continuation, but Black should not stop analysing here, as there are still many 'only moves' to be made: 27.♔a1 ♕e6 28.♖h1 ♔e7 29.♕c5+ ♔d7 30.♖d1+ ♔c7 31.♖d6 ♕e8, and despite White's serious initiative there is no way to win the game if Black plays accurately.

**26.♔b1 ♔f8 27.♕d6+**

**27...♔g8**

The only – and decisive – mistake. 27...♔g7 was a necessity, but the reason is not obvious. So, either you remember this or it's very difficult to figure out the correct way over the board: 28.♕e7 c5 (the only move) 29.♔a1 ♖a6!

ANALYSIS DIAGRAM

and here comes the difference! With the king on g8, White wins by giving a check on the back rank, while in the current position there's no ♖d8 check and Black's rook is just in time to defend the king. Do you remember the strange-looking 24... a5 ? Only now do you realize why Black needed it. After 30.♕g5+ ♖g6 31.♕xf5 ♖g1 32.♕f6+ ♔g8 (or 32...♔f8) 33.♖xg1+ ♕xg1+ 34.♔a2 it's a draw.

**28.♕e7**

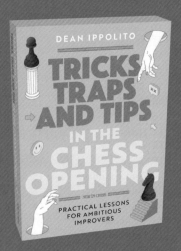
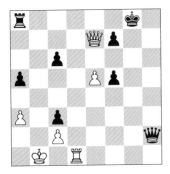

I knew this position was winning, but the pressure of the last round, the importance of the match and fatigue affected me negatively. So, I decided to spend more time before making

## 'I knew this position was winning, but the importance of the match and fatigue affected me negatively'

each of my next moves, rechecking all the calculated lines, so as not to let the advantage slip through my fingers.
**28...♕f2 29.♔a1**

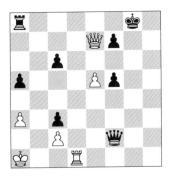

The only winning move, but also a very logical one. The threat of ...♕b6-b2 mate was very annoying.
**29...♕g2** Preventing ♕g5 and controlling the h1-square, but Black's king is just too weak and White launches a devastating attack.
**30.e6**

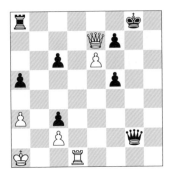

**30...fxe6**
Also losing was 30...♖f8 31.exf7+ ♖xf7 32.♕d8+ ♔g7 33.♕e5+ ♖f6 34.♖d7+ ♔g6 35.♕e8+ ♔h6 36.♕h8+ ♔g5 37.♖g7+ ♖g6 38.♖xg6+ ♔xg6 39.♕g8+.
**31.♕xe6+ ♔h8**

**32.♕xf5** An easy-looking move, but not so easy to play.
I thought about 32.♖d7, with several mating ideas, but could not find how to continue after 32...♕g5, while 32.♕f6+ ♔g8 33.♖d7 would be a huge mistake, as I don't control the c4-square: 33...♕f1+ 34.♔a2 ♕c4+, with a perpetual.
**32...♖a7 33.♖d8+ ♔g7 34.♕f8+ ♔g6 35.♖d6+**

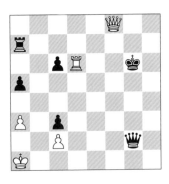

Black resigned.

NOTES BY
**Anna Muzychuk**

**Anna Muzychuk**
**Gergana Peycheva**
Chennai Olympiad 2022 (4)
French Defence, Winawer Variation

The 44th Olympiad in Chennai will always be remembered, and will always remain in our hearts and minds. I and most of my teammates became Olympic Champions for the first time in our lives. In 2018, at the Olympiad in Baku, I won a gold medal by showing the best performance on Board 1, but winning a gold medal with the team is even more special.

This game is not the best game I played in Chennai, but I find it the most exciting one, with quite a few instructional moments.

**1.e4 e6 2.d4 d5 3.♘c3 ♘f6 4.e5 ♘fd7 5.f4 c5 6.♘f3 ♘c6 7.♗e3 a6 8.♘e2**

I have played many games in this line, but this was the first time I opted for 8.♘e2, deviating from the main 8.♕d2. Of course, there's nothing wrong with 8.♕d2. Besides, I also

tried 8.a3 – prophylaxis against ...b5-b4, and sometimes with the idea of dxc5, followed by b4. There are also quite a lot of games with 8.♗e2, preparing castling kingside.

As we can see, all the moves have totally different ideas. The idea of ♘e2 is to strengthen the d4-square by playing c3 and then start an attack on the kingside by preparing f5. But we can also see a clear drawback of this move – the e2-knight blocks the f1-bishop and prevents its development. Luckily, the centre is closed, so we have some time for manoeuvring.

**8...b5** In my opinion, this is already an inaccuracy. It kind of looks logical, as it's clear that White's play is on the kingside and Black's on the

queenside, but the knight has left the c3-square.

Many strong grandmasters preferred 8...♕b6, which I think is a better move. Black is trying to highlight White's lack of coordination. After 9.♕c1 f6 (a concrete approach, trying to open the centre) 10.c3 ♗e7 White has a choice: to simplify the position with 11.exf6 ♘xf6 12.dxc5 ♗xc5 13.♗xc5 ♕xc5 14.♘ed4 and have a slight advantage due to the better bishop and the better pawn structure, or get involved in a complicated struggle starting with 11.h4. In the latter case, White continues with h5-h6, sometimes followed by the creative ♖h3-g3.

**9.c3 ♗b7**

**10.g4**

Logical but maybe not the best. The engines prefer 10.♘g3, but I wasn't sure how to continue after 10...g6. Now we cannot break through with f5 without sacrificing a piece.

I also considered 10.dxc5 ♘xc5 11.♘ed4, followed by easy development, although with dxc5 White releases the pressure and creates more space – both for their own pieces and for Black. It's difficult to say who benefits more from this.

**10...♕b6**

If we look at this position more deeply, we may find some similarity with the King's Indian Defence. The sides are mirrored but the ideas remain similar. For example, after 10...h5 White simply takes 11.gxh5 and after 11...♖xh5 we will play 12.h4, just as in the KID – when Black meets White's b4 with ...a5, White has the

idea to take on a5, then play a4, ♞b3 and continue with c5 or a5.

**11.♞g3?** Nice and... wrong ☺. I thought about opening the diagonal for the bishop and put the knight on g3, so that I don't have to think about ...h5 anymore. But in reality the knight on g3 is a bit misplaced. It had to control the d4-square, or after f5 jump to f4. Therefore 11.♗h3 or 11.♗g2 would have been better.
11.f5? is very premature as 11...♞cxe5 12.dxe5 d4 favours Black.

**11...♗e7?**

Black missed a very good moment to open the game: 11...cxd4! 12.cxd4 ♗b4+ 13.♚e2 0-0-0, followed by ...f6. As in the line with 8...♛b6, we can see that the correct way to play this position from Black's side is to try to open the centre as soon as possible, before White coordinates their pieces and finishes the development.

**12.♗d3 0-0-0 13.0-0 ♚b8 14.♛d2**

This looks like a normal move – connecting the rooks, protecting the bishop on e3 and so preparing f5. At the same time, the queen is not well placed on d2 in some lines.
14.h4, 14.♗f2, or 14.a3 were interesting alternatives.

The roller-coaster game that Anna Muzychuk won against Gergana Peycheva ended with a bright smile, as all is well that ends well!

LENNART OOTES

**14...h6?** This is definitely wrong. Black weakens the important g6-square. After f5 and the trade on e6, White will have a clear plan to bring the knight to g6.
14...g6 was undoubtedly stronger: 15.♖ab1 (after 15.a3 cxd4 16.cxd4 ♞a5 we see the problem of the queen on d2) 15...cxd4 16.cxd4 h5 17.gxh5 gxh5 18.b4, when White is slightly better.

**15.f5 ♖df8**

**16.♖f2**

16.♞h5 was premature in view of 16...g6 17.fxg6? fxg6 18.♞f4 (18.♗xg6 ♖hg8) 18...cxd4 19.cxd4 ♖xf4 20.♗xf4 ♞xd4, and Black is clearly better.

16.h3!? and 16.♗f2 were nice prophylactic moves.

**16...cxd4?! 17.cxd4 ♗d8**

**18.♖af1?**

Another important moment. I saw that Black's idea was to regroup her pieces with ...♛a7 and ...♗b6, putting more pressure on the d4- and e5-pawns, but didn't react correctly. I had miscalculated the line that I played and I was very sad about my decision at this point, because now I saw the correct continuation.
The move I really wanted to make was 18.b4!, as now ...♛a7 simply does not work. But I did not like that after 18...♗e7 (18...♛a7? fails to 19.a4 bxa4

20.b5, and Black is in trouble) I have to put my rook on b1, 19.♖b1, where it will have to stay, and not on f1, where I had intended to place it.

But, on the other hand, Black has no plans now. If 19...♕a7, then White is faster on the kingside: 20.♘h5 g6 21.fxg6 fxg6 22.♘f4 ♖xf4 23.♗xf4 ♘xd4 24.♘xd4 ♕xd4 25.♗xg6, and White is winning.

**18...♕a7 19.fxe6?**

Better was 19.♗b1 ♗b6 20.♔g2, with a white advantage.

**19...fxe6 20.♘h5?**

Continuing the line that I started with 18.♖af1, but all this is very wrong.

**20...♗b6**

Inserting 20...♗a5 21.♕e2 is not good for Black, because after 21...♗b6 White takes 22.♘xg7, and after all the trades on d4 I can take on e6. With the queen on e2, the g4-pawn is protected.

**21.♗b1 ♖xf3**

Interesting was 21...g5!? 22.♔g2 ♖c8, followed by ...♖hf8.

**22.♖xf3 ♘xd4 23.♖f7 ♘xe5 24.♖f8+ ♖xf8 25.♖xf8+**

After lots of complications and sacri-

fices we have another critical position. Black is under check and has only two moves. One is losing and the other one leads to a completely unclear position. How would you play?

**25...♔c7?** 25...♗c8 was correct: 26.♔g2 ♘c4 27.♕f2 e5, and it's difficult to say who is better. In a practical game maybe I would prefer Black.

**26.♔g2**

The problem for Black is that in this line the king on c7 is more exposed, and the queen on a7 is more out of play compared to the lines after 25...♗c8. But I can understand why Black decided to play 25...♔c7: on b7 the bishop has more potential than on c8 and is not pinned.

**26...♘c4 27.♕f2 ♗c5**

**28.♕f7+?**

It was very tempting to take pawns with check, but it was more important to keep the king in the 'danger zone' with 28.♖f7+ ♔b8 29.♖xg7. During the game I did not feel as if it was +6, but when you look at the position more closely, it's clear that Black is just collapsing: 29...♘xe3+ 30.♕xe3 ♕b6 31.♘f6, threatening ♘d7+.

**28...♔b6 29.♗xd4 ♗xd4**

**30.♕xe6+?**

30.♘xg7 was much stronger.

**30...♔a5**

And... the king has come to a5, where it suddenly feels safe. And... everything is unclear again ☺.

**31.♘f4 ♗xb2 32.♖f7?**

This doesn't look so bad visually, but it could have cost me the game.

32.♘d3 was necessary, with an unclear position.

**32...♕d4?**

Here 32...♗e5 was very strong, when there is no defence against ...♕e3, and Black would be winning.

**33.♘d3**

And now, after this knight retreat, the position is equal again.

# A tell-all book about Spassky-Fischer 1972

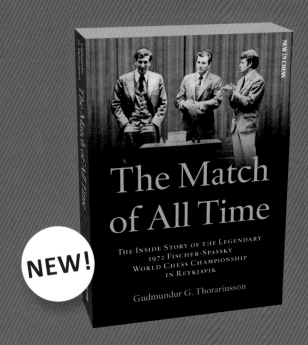

**NEW!**

The 1972 'Match of All Time' between Bobby Fischer and Boris Spassky was probably the most iconic sports contest during the Cold War. Fifty years on, the organizer of the match Gudmundur Thorarinsson, who was president of the Icelandic Chess Federation, has written a tell-all book about the match, crammed with behind-the-scenes stories and improbable twists and turns.

# Smart Choices in the Opening

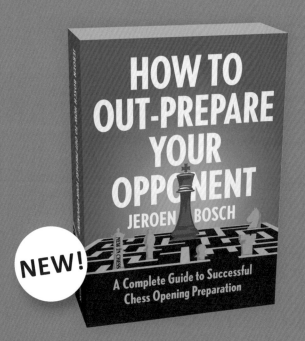

**NEW!**

International Master **Jeroen Bosch** gives you all the tools you need to dominate the opening phase of the game. He presents a structured approach to the study of openings and the preparation for a club match or a tournament game. Instead of studying more hours or memorizing more lines, you have to make smart choices. The goal is to dictate what will happen on the board. You want to get a position you understand and like to play – and at the same time make your opponent feel uncomfortable

**33...♗c8?**

Another big mistake in time-trouble, and this was the last one. Black had hoped for perpetual check, but I have quite a lot of pieces to repel the threats.

33...♗c6 was possible, since taking the bishop would lead to a loss for White after 34.♕xc6? ♕xg4+ 35.♔f1 ♕d1+ 36.♔g2 ♘e3+.

**34.♕xc8 ♕e4+ 35.♖f3 ♕e2+ 36.♖f2 ♕e4+ 37.♖f3**

To gain time on the clock I was just repeating moves.

**37...♕e2+ 38.♔g3**

**38...♗e5+**

From a practical point of view 38...♗d4 would have been much more dangerous. In that case only two moves win – 39.♕f8 and 39.♕c7+ ♔a4 40.♕f4.

**39.♘xe5 ♕xe5+ 40.♔h3**

The rest is easy.

**40...h5 41.♗f5 g6 42.♗xg6 hxg4+ 43.♕xg4 ♘e3 44.♕f4 ♕h8+ 45.♔g3 d4 46.h4**

Black resigned.

A roller-coaster game, which could have ended in different results, but as they say – all is well that ends well. ☺

## Gold medal Board 1

The best result on Board 1 in the Women's Olympiad was a contest between highly experienced Pia Cramling from Sweden and 16-year-old Dutch debutant Eline Roebers. Remarkably, both had exactly the same rating performance – 2532 – but as Cramling had played all games and Roebers had had to sit out a round because of illness, the Swedish star won the gold medal, while the Dutch rising star took silver.

Fortunately, both agreed to look back on their Chennai experience.

**NOTES BY**
**Pia Cramling**

**Pia Cramling**
**Eline Roebers**
Chennai Olympiad 2022 (9)
Dutch Defence, Leningrad Variation

Before Chennai, Zhaoqin Peng of the Netherlands sent me a message and asked me how many Olympiads I had played. She thought I would beat her record of 16 (!) Olympiads if Chennai was included. Even though my debut was a long time ago, I have not always played, and I am happy to have participated 13 times during the years; nine of them were with the Swedish Women's team (the other times she played in the Open Section – ed.). I play for the national team because I enjoy it so much. We have a great spirit in the team, and the best is when my daughter Anna takes part, as she did in Baku and Chennai. My husband Juan has been the captain every time I played since 2002, and he was also in Turin 2006, when I did not take part. To have him in the team as a captain means very much to me.

Of all the Olympiads I have played, this was the number one. The hotel, the gym I visited every day, the food, the playing venue with the cold playing halls were excellent. I appreciated the way they had made the two playing halls with both the Open teams and the Women's teams together, so that I could see friends and games from both events. The organizers' concern for the players and everyone who was part of the Olympiad was overwhelming. One day it took me almost an hour and a half to reach the hotel after my game instead of the regular half an hour, as I took a minibus that stopped at different hotels. When I arrived, the organizers had already started a search for me to make sure that I was safe.

We were rated 34 in the starting list and the team did very well, playing 7 out of 11 matches against higher rated teams. But losing the last two rounds was crucial and sent us down to 40th place, which was below our initial starting rank.

One of the most exciting matches we had was the encounter against the Netherlands in Round 9, which finished 2-2. In the end, we should have won, as Peng played too riskily, running across the board with her king, for which she could have been punished by Inna Agrest, who scored a great result in the Olympiad on Board 2 for us.

Young Eline Roebers, the new upcoming star, was my opponent. She is about the same age I was when I played my first Olympiad in Buenos Aires in 1978! I was happy

## 'My husband Juan has been the captain every time I played since 2002. To have him in the team as a captain means very much to me'

that my overall result was enough to take the gold medal on 1st board, and it was Anna who told me about it after the final round! Curiously enough, it was a race between Eline Roebers and me that decided the gold and silver medals. It was only because I had played all my 11 games that I could pass her, because she had played one game less.

We had the same performance rating: 2532...

**1.d4 f5**

I had not expected my opponent to go for the Dutch, but of course for a player from the Netherlands this must be the obvious choice!

**2.g3 ♘f6 3.♗g2 g6 4.♘f3 ♗g7 5.0-0 0-0 6.b3**

My pet line against the Dutch, which I have played for more than 20 years. I was curious to see what my opponent had prepared against me.

**6...d6 7.♗b2 ♘e4**

Here it comes. A move that, if I remember correctly, used to be quite popular a long time back, but lost its popularity when White started playing 9.♘e1, as in the game.

**8.♘bd2 ♘c6**

| Board Medals – Women | | |
| --- | --- | --- |
| **Board 1** | | |
| Gold | **Pia Cramling** | SWE |
| Silver | **Eline Roebers** | NED |
| Bronze | **Zhansaya Abdumalik** | KAZ |
| **Board 2** | | |
| Gold | **Nino Batsiashvili** | GEO |
| Silver | **Anna Muzychuk** | UKR |
| Bronze | **Khanim Balajayeva** | AZE |
| **Board 3** | | |
| Gold | **Oliwia Kiolbasa** | POL |
| Silver | **Anna Ushenina** | UKR |
| Bronze | **Vaishali R** | IND |
| **Board 4** | | |
| Gold | **Bat-Erdene Mungunzul** | MNG |
| Silver | **Maria Malicka** | POL |
| Bronze | **Tania Sachdev** | IND |
| **Board 5** | | |
| Gold | **Jana Schneider** | GER |
| Silver | **Ulviyya Fataliyeva** | AZE |
| Bronze | **Deshmukh Divya** | IND-2 |

**9.♘e1**

The knight retreat forces Black to decide what to do with the knight on e4.

Another way to handle the position is to allow Black to get the pawn break ...e7-e5: 9.c4!? ♘xd2 10.♕xd2 e5 11.dxe5 dxe5 12.♕d5+ ♔h8 13.♕xd8 ♖xd8 14.♘g5. Many games have been played this way, and Black's most popular continuation has been 14...♖d2.

**9...♘g5**

Probably the best option. Black keeps the knight on the board without giving up the e5-square.

It is well known that White gets a nice position if Black continues 9...♘xd2 10.♕xd2 e5 11.♗d5+ ♔h8 12.♗xc6 bxc6 13.dxe5 dxe5 14.♘d3.

9...d5 was played against me by Helgi Dam Ziska in Calvia 2006, but after 10.♘df3 Black will no longer be able to play ...e7-e5.

**10.f4 ♘f7 11.♘c4**

Again White intends to discourage Black from playing ...e7-e5.

**11...e6 12.e3 ♖b8 13.a4 ♘e7 14.♘d3 b6**

A logical plan – exchanging my active bishop on g2 for Black's passive bishop. Black can also choose to do it with ...♗d7-c6 but to me ...b6, to keep the ...c5 option open, looks more natural.

**15.♕e2 ♗b7 16.♗xb7 ♖xb7 17.♘d2**

My plan was to keep the pieces in the centre and try to open up the position later on with either e4 or c4, followed by d5.

**17...♖b8 18.♘f3 ♖e8**

In her 13th Olympiad, Pia Cramling won the gold medal on Board 1. In a key game the Swedish star defeated Eline Roebers of the Netherlands, who is about the same age as she was when she played her first Olympiad in Buenos Aires in 1978!

One is 28.♕f6, to follow up with ♘h4, but choosing to go for an attack may require exact play, and a mistake might be punished severely. White can also choose a more solid continuation with, for example 28.♖xe8+ ♖xe8 29.♘h4 ♘h6 30.bxa4, when White's pieces are better placed than Black's. Especially Black's two knights on the rim are not easy to activate. White has a large advantage. 22...exd5?! makes it easier for White: 23.♗xg7! ♔xg7 24.cxd5, and White has a clear advantage, planning ♘f2, followed by e4. The fact that the king is on g7 benefits White. It is important that 24...♘d4?? does not work: 25.♕b2!, and the knight is pinned.
**22...e5**

The pawn break that Black was aiming for when playing ...♘c6.
**23.d5 e4!** 23...♘e7? 24.e4!, and White opens up the position: 24...fxe4 25.♖xe4 ♘f5 26.♖de1, putting maximum pressure on Black.
**24.♗xg7**

After a long think. Black decides to keep an eye on the e6-pawn and is also planning to push the e-pawn further as soon as she can.
**19.c4 c5 20.♖ad1 ♕c7 21.♖fe1 ♘c6?**
Black is playing to achieve ...e5, but gives me a chance to open up the centre, which benefits White.
21...♖bd8!? was more cautious, and Black remains solid.

Black to avoid having the king on g7, as it gives more flexibility to White) 23.♕xb2 exd5 24.cxd5.
Only if Black now replies ...♘b4 will White exchange the knight and play on the weak squares in Black's camp. After other knight moves the natural plan for White is to play ♘f2 and push the e-pawn, to open up the e-file and the position in front of Black's king. For instance: 24...♘a5!? 25.♘f2 b5 (to create counterplay on the queenside) 26.e4! bxa4 27.exf5 gxf5.

**22.♕c2?!** Preparing to play d5 on the next move, but I could have played it right away.
The obvious 22.d5! was my first idea, but I did not realize how strong it was: 22...♗xb2! (it is preferable for

**ANALYSIS DIAGRAM**

White's initiative is more dangerous, but the position is sharp. White can choose different ways to continue.

**24...♔xg7** The natural response, and my opponent also played it immediately.. After 24...exd3, 25.♕c3! is strong. Here Black will

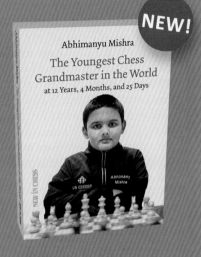
have to be concerned about the long open diagonal: 25...♘b4 26.♗f6 ♘c2 27.♕xd3 ♘xe1 28.♖xe1, and White has more than enough compensation for the exchange.

**25.dxc6**

**25...exf3**

I had expected Black to take the other knight, as my pieces coordinate better now. But Black is fine here, too. After 25...exd3, 26.♖xd3 ♕xc6 27.♖d5 ♖e6 28.e4 was my plan. The queen is excellent on c2, defending e4 and has the intermediate move ♕c3+, if necessary, to change diagonal or defend the rook on e1. Now 28...fxe4! is a natural and strong move. After 29.f5!? gxf5 30.♘h4, chances are equal.

**26.♘f2** Logical – getting rid of my backward pawn and opening up the centre with e4.

**26...♖e6?**

A mistake that gives White the chance to take the initiative when the e-file opens.

26...♕xc6! 27.e4, and now the calm 27...♘h6, defending f5, would have given Black equal chances.

**27.e4**

The problem for Black is that there are too many threats and there is no good way to defend against them all. Black's pieces are not coordinating well.

**27...♖be8**

27...fxe4 allows White to bring the knight into Black's position: 28.♕c3+ ♔f8 29.♘xe4 ♖be8 30.♘f6 ♖xe1+ 31.♖xe1 ♖xe1+ 32.♕xe1 ♕xc6 33.♘xh7+ ♔g7 34.♕e7 ♔xh7 35.♕xf7+ ♔h8 36.♕xg6, and White is winning.

If 27...♕xc6 then 28.exf5 ♖xe1+ 29.♖xe1 d5! 30.fxg6 hxg6 31.cxd5 ♕xd5 32.♕c3+ ♔f8 33.♖e4, and White will eventually win the f3-pawn.

And 27...♘h6 is not so good now: 28.♕c3+ ♔g8 29.exf5 ♖xe1+ 30.♖xe1 ♘xf5 31.♘g4! ♘d4 32.♘f6+ ♔h8 33.♘d5 ♕xc6 34.♖e7, and White gets an extremely strong position and will follow up with ♕e1.

**28.♕c3+ ♔f8 29.exf5**

**29...♖xe1+** 29...♖e2 was preferable, although 30.fxg6 hxg6 31.♖xe2 fxe2 32.♖e1 ♕xc6 33.♕d3 will leave White with an extra pawn.

**30.♖xe1 ♖xe1+ 31.♕xe1 gxf5 32.♕e6**

**32...♕e7** Giving White no choice but to enter the knight endgame, but it is good enough.

After 32...♕xc6 33.♕xf5 ♕e8 34.♘e4 ♔g7 35.♔f2 White is dominating the position completely.

**33.♕xe7+**

Not 33.♕c8+?? ♔g7, and Black wins!

**33...♔xe7 34.♘d1**

Activating the knight and using the hole on d5 and the weakness on f5. There is no way that Black can both win the c6-pawn and defend her own f5-pawn. The poor knight on f7 has no way to enter the game actively.

**34...♔e6** Or 34...♔d8 35.♘e3 ♘h6 36.♘d5, planning h3 and ♔f2.

**35.♘e3 ♘h6 36.♔f2 ♘g8 37.♘d5**

Black resigned.

NOTES BY
**Eline Roebers**

**Julia Ryjanova**
**Eline Roebers**
Chennai Olympiad 2022 (11)
King's Indian, Fianchetto Variation

My first ever Olympiad was a successful one for me personally. Going into the last round, I had already won about 45 rating points and completed the last IM norm needed for the title.

In the final round, the Netherlands were playing Australia. Team-wise, there wasn't much to play for except the difference between a bad tournament and a decent one. I was still competing for a board medal and wanted to finish the tournament on a good note after losing a bad game to legend Pia Cramling (who ended up taking the gold medal on Board 1 with an incredible 9½/11) in Round 9 and taking a round off in Round 10. I was ready for a fight!

**1.d4 ♘f6 2.c4 g6 3.♘f3 ♗g7 4.g3**

Before the game, I had seen that Julia had recently opted for Catalans and Fianchetto systems, so this didn't come as a surprise.

**4...0-0 5.♗g2 d6 6.0-0 ♘c6 7.♘c3 a6 8.b3 ♖b8 9.d5 ♘a5**

**10.♗d2**

In Round 5, I had faced 10.♗g5, after which I had prepared a rare piece sacrifice line (only played five times before, according to my database) and won a pretty good game. For my preparation I had focused on finding

an alternative to this line and hadn't had time to check the other lines, as the round already started at 10 am. So from this point onwards, I was on my own.

My game in Round 5 saw 10.♗g5 b5 11.cxb5 axb5 12.b4 c5 13.bxa5 ♕xa5 14.♖c1 b4 15.♗xf6 ♗xf6 16.♘e4 ♗g7 17.♕b3 ♗d7 18.♘ed2 ♖a8 19.♖a1 ♕a3 20.♖ab1 ♕xa2 21.♖fc1 ♕xb3 22.♖xb3 ♖a2

**ANALYSIS DIAGRAM**

23.e3 ♗a4 24.♖bb1 ♗c2, and Black was winning (0-1, 70) in Frayna-Roebers, Chennai 2022.

**10...c5 11.dxc6 ♘xc6 12.♖c1**

**12...♗e6**

12...♗f5 is the main move, which is slightly more accurate than the text (although the theory suggests that White should be better anyway).

**13.♘g5 ♗d7 14.♘ge4 ♘e8**

14...♘xe4 would have been a better move. Black has less space and would like to exchange pieces. Still, White has a slight edge after 15.♘xe4 ♘e5 16.♗c3. I didn't like my winning chances in this position, so went for the more complicated option, although I'm sure this would have

been objectively better than the game continuation

**15.♘d5**
This is still better for White, but at least it walks into my plan.
15.c5! would have been difficult to deal with for Black. E.g. 15...f5 16.♘g5 e6 17.cxd6 h6 18.♗xc6 bxc6 19.♘f3 e5 20.♗e3, when Black can't make use of the light squares and can't win back the d6-pawn.
**15...f5 16.♘g5**
16.♘ec3 is better, with the idea of a quick e4. Now I get to hunt the knights back and equalize.
**16...e6 17.♘c3 h6 18.♘h3**

**18...♘e5?**
This, however, is a mistake. I was too focused on playing ...b5 or ...♗c6. My opponent now comes with a strong follow-up. After 18...e5 19.♘d5 ♗e6 Black is totally fine.
**19.e4 b5**
I finally get to push ...b5, but my centre becomes slightly awkward.
**20.cxb5 axb5 21.exf5 gxf5 22.♘f4 ♘f6 23.♘ce2 b4 24.♘d4**
All very strong play by my opponent.
**24...♖e8**

**25.♘c2** Too materialistic, as this allows Black to get the desired ...♘e4 in and equalize, with White having the difficult position.
25.♖e1 would have been a strong and natural move, paralysing my centre and leaving me without a good plan. During the game I thought I would have ...♘e4 ideas, but they turned out pretty hard to realise, as you can't get the light-squared bishop on the h1-a8 diagonal.
**25...♘e4 26.♗xb4 ♗b5 27.♖e1 ♛b6**

Now f2 is a target and the knight on e4 should be removed.
**28.♗xe4?**
The engine thinks White is objectively okay here, but giving up the light-squared bishop is a strategic blunder and makes defending quite difficult for White.
I only calculated taking with the rook, and I came to the conclusion that it would lead to unclear play: 28.♖xe4! fxe4 29.♗xe4 d5 30.♗g2 ♖bc8, when Black is playing for ideas like ...d4. The computer claims that White has an edge, but with time-pressure and a messy position in general, anything can happen.

16-year-old Eline Roebers had a marvellous Olympiad debut, gaining 50 rating points, making her final IM norm and winning silver on Board 1, only a hair's breadth behind Pia Cramling.

**33.♔f1 ♛h1+ 34.♔e2 ♗f3+ 35.♖xf3 ♛xf3+ 36.♔f1 ♛h1+ 37.♔e2 ♛e4+ 38.♘e3 ♖a8 39.♔xd6 ♖xa2+ 40.♖c2 ♖xc2+ 41.♛xc2 ♛f3+ 42.♔f1 ♛xh5**

The rest is no longer important.
**43.♛c7 ♛xh2 44.♛b7** Or 44.♗xe5 ♛h1+ 45.♔e2 ♛h5+, and ...♗xe5 next. **44...♛h3+ 45.♔e1 ♛h5 46.♔f1 ♛f3 47.♛b5 ♖c8 48.♔e1 ♖c1+ 49.♔d2 ♛xf2+ 50.♔xc1 ♛xe3+ 51.♔c2 ♛e4+ 52.♔c1 ♘d3+ 53.♔d2 ♛e1+**

And as 54.♔xd3 loses to 54...♛f1+, my opponent resigned.
With this win we beat Australia 3-1 and finished in 20th place, which is an okay result. I also won the silver medal on Board 1. ∎

**28...fxe4**

**29.♖xe4?**

This allows Black to get a very strong light-squared bishop on the long h1-a8 diagonal.
29.♖e3!, along with sacrificing the exchange on the next move, is the only way to hold the balance (one move earlier, this would have been more effective, since White would have got to keep her light-squared bishop). After 29...♘f3+ 30.♖xf3 exf3 31.♛xf3 White should play for Black's weaknesses on the kingside.
**29...♗c6 30.♖e3**

White should have played 30.♖xe5!

dxe5 (30...♗xe5?) 31.♘h5 ♗a8 32.♛g4 ♛b7 33.♛xg7+ ♛xg7 34.♘xg7 ♔xg7 35.♗c3.
**30...♗a8!**

Not a difficult move, but a very strong one, as it prepares the bishop-queen battery.
**31.♘h5**

31.♔f1 would have kept the damage to a minimum, but White has to be careful regardless.
**31...♗h8**

31...♖f8 was even stronger.
**32.♗a3 ♛b7**

And the threats along the diagonal are deadly.

A 'very happy and relieved' Magnus Carlsen secured victory in the FTX Crypto Cup and then lost his next three games against Pragg.

# Magnus wins in Miami

## World Champion strengthens lead in Meltwater Champions Tour

The FTX Crypto Cup, the second Major of the Meltwater Champions Chess Tour, saw Magnus Carlsen extend his overall lead. The World Champion took first place in Miami, despite a last-round loss to rising star Praggnanandhaa. **PETER HEINE NIELSEN** takes a closer look at a game with an unusual finish and two remarkable fragments.

NOTES BY
**Peter Heine Nielsen**

**Anish Giri**
**Magnus Carlsen**
Miami FTX Crypto Cup 2022 (1.3)
French Defence, Advance Variation

**1.e4**
Anish Giri starts with the most aggressive move.
**1...e6!?**
The French. A peculiar choice by Magnus, perhaps paying tribute to the only second who was with him for all his five World Championship matches, Laurent Fressinet.
**2.d4 d5 3.e5!?**
Typical of modern chess. In older times, one would consider 3.♘c3 more ' 'principled', but these days this often leads to long forcing lines, so the attention has switched to approaches in which White more

aims for playable positions of a less forcing nature.

**3...c5 4.c3 ♘c6 5.♘f3 ♗d7!?**
5...♕b6 used to be the main line, but Magnus himself (re-)introduced 6.♗d3 cxd4 7.0-0 – a pawn sacrifice recommended by the neural networks. That cutting-edge artificial intelligence should conclude that Jonny Hector's pawn sacrifice was sound did indeed come as a surprise to me, but hats off to the creative Swede!

**6.♗e2 ♘ge7 7.0-0 cxd4 8.cxd4 ♘f5 9.♘c3 ♖c8**

Another typical opening scenario, with the position being a mini 'zugzwang' situation. Black's natural developing move 9...♗e7 is met by 10.g4!, and since Black would much rather recapture on h4 with his queen after 10...♘h4 11.♘xh4, he has to keep waiting and make semi-useful moves in the meantime.

**10.♔h1!? a6! 11.♗g5**

Giri gets tired of waiting,

**11...♖b6 12.♘a4 ♕a7**

**13.♗e3**

The conventional move, defending the d4-pawn. 13.g4!? would have been more creative, with Black having to resort to tactics like 13...♘cxd4

The FTX Crypto Cup was the sixth leg and the second major of the Meltwater Champions Tour. In Miami, Florida, 8 players competed in a 7-round rapid all-play-all. Sitting opposite each other, but essentially playing online.

Each round consisted of a 4-game mini-match, in case of a tie followed by a blitz tiebreak and if necessary an Armageddon game. A straight win earned 3 points; a win in the tiebreak: 2 points; a loss in the tiebreak: 1 point.

14.gxf5 ♘xe2, keeping the balance in a complex fight, since 15.♕xe2 ♗xa4 is possible.

**13...♗e7**

As he is now able to meet 14.g4 with 14...♘xe3, Black can return to normality and finish his development.

**14.a3 b5 15.♘c3 0-0 16.♗d3 ♘xe3 17.fxe3 b4 18.axb4 ♘xb4**

Strategically an interesting position. Magnus's a-pawn looks weak, and White potentially has a kingside attack, both due to the f-file and his space advantage with the pawn on e5. But the bishop pair might easily compensate for all of that!

**19.e4?**

The real culprit. After 19.♗b1 White's position would not be too bad. However, Giri does not want to ease the pressure on the a6-pawn.

**19...♘xd3 20.♕xd3 dxe4 21.♘xe4 h6!**

The key point. White was threatening 22.♘eg5, forcing ...g6 due to the threat of mate on h7. This would leave the dark squares around the black king, especially f6 and h6, weakened. 21...♗b5? obviously fails to 22.♕xb5!, but Magnus again has evaluated deeper, and quietly protects his kingside structure, understanding that after 22.♖xa6 ♕b8 he will regain the pawn due to numerous threats, and keep his positional edge as well.

**22.♖fe1 a5 23.♕d2 ♗c6 24.♕f4**

24.♘f6+ was possible, but Black can just happily ignore it and play 24...♔h8.

**24...♕b8 25.♖e2 a4 26.♕g4 ♕b5 27.♖ae1 ♗b4!**

Safer ways were possible, but Magnus correctly trusts that White has no mate, and decides to pick up material.

## Miami FTX Crypto Cup 2022

| | | rapid elo | 1 | 2 | 3 | 4 | 5 | 6 | 7 | 8 | |
|---|---|---|---|---|---|---|---|---|---|---|---|
| 1 | Carlsen | 2834 | – | 1 (2-4) | 2 (3½-2½) | 3 (3-1) | 1 (2-4) | 3 (2½-1½) | 3 (3-1) | 3 (3-1) | 16 |
| 2 | Praggnanandhaa | - | 2 (4-2) | – | 3 (2½-1½) | 0 (½-2½) | 1 (2-4) | 3 (3-1) | 3 (2½-1½) | 3 (2½-1½) | 15 |
| 3 | Firouzja | 2704 | 1 (2½-3½) | 0 (1½-2½) | – | 3 (2½-½) | 3 (2½-1½) | 3 (2½-1½) | 2 (4-3) | 3 (2½-½) | 15 |
| 4 | Le Quang Liem | 2661 | 0 (1-3) | 3 (2½-½) | 0 (½-2½) | – | 3 (2½-½) | 0 (1½-2½) | 3 (2½-½) | 3 (2½-1½) | 12 |
| 5 | Duda | 2808 | 2 (4-2) | 2 (4-2) | 0 (1½-2½) | 0 (½-2½) | – | 1 (2½-3½) | 3 (2½-½) | 3 (3-0) | 11 |
| 6 | Aronian | 2728 | 0 (1½-2½) | 0 (1-3) | 0 (1½-2½) | 3 (2½-1½) | 2 (3½-2½) | – | 0 (½-2½) | 3 (2½-1½) | 8 |
| 7 | Giri | 2721 | 0 (1-3) | 0 (1½-2½) | 1 (3-4) | 0 (½-2½) | 0 (½-2½) | 3 (2½-½) | – | 3 (2½-1½) | 7 |
| 8 | Niemann | 2529 | 0 (1-3) | 0 (1½-2½) | 0 (½-2½) | 0 (1½-2½) | 0 (0-3) | 0 (1½-2½) | 0 (1½-2½) | – | 0 |

**28.d5!?** My favourite illustrative line is 28.♘f6+ ♚h8 29.♘h5 ♖g8! 30.♘g5 ♗e8!?. **28...♖xe1 29.♘d4 ♕d3 30.♖xe1 ♗xd5 31.♘f6+ ♚h8 32.♘xd5 ♕d2!?**

Computer-like precision, but Magnus had undoubtedly spotted the nice trick that will end this game now, and was hoping to be able to display an unusual mating motif.

**33.♖d1 ♖c1 34.♘c3**

Here I calculated the trivial win 34...♖xd1+ 35.♕xd1 ♕xd1+ 36.♘xd1 ♖d8!. Winning it is, charming it's not. Magnus's next move, on the other hand, made the chess world smile.

**34...♕e1+!**

Elegant and unusual. A nice version of the back rank mate.

Hans Niemann speaks the epic words 'Chess speaks for itself' after he won his first game against Magnus Carlsen.

**Hans Niemann**
**Magnus Carlsen**
Miami FTX Crypto Cup 2022 (2.4)

position after 11.♘b5

In the first game of the match, Hans Niemann played an excellent game, followed by an equally impressive 'chess speaks for itself' interview. But Magnus worked his way back into the match, and now only needed a draw to clinch it.

At this point, he missed a fairly easy tactic, as he himself admitted after the game. Indeed, 11...a6!, with the idea of 12.♘xc7? ♖a7!, trapping the stranded knight, has been seen before.

**11...♗a6?! 12.♗f4 ♖c8 13.a4**

♗b7 **14.a5?!** Tempting, especially having seen the upcoming tactic.

**14...a6 15.axb6 axb5 16.♖a7!?** This looks cool, as after 16...♖xa7 17.bxa7 White wins back the piece because Black cannot evacuate the b8-knight without removing the protection of its colleague on d7.

## In the first game of the match, Hans Niemann played an excellent game, followed by an equally impressive 'chess speaks for itself' interview

And as 16...♗c6? 17.b7! is even worse, one can understand why Hans was attracted to this tactic. But...

**16...♘xb6! 17.♖xb7 ♘c6!**
Although Magnus had missed trapping the c7-knight, he did spot trapping the b7-rook! There is no escaping from ...♘a5 or ...♘d8 next. Hans fought on, but the result of the game and thus the match was never in doubt.

**18.♗xb5 ♘a5**
And Black won (0-1, 31).

LENNART OOTES

**Praggnanandhaa was in the right mood in Miami after his splendid 2767 performance at the Olympiad.**

# Talent, surely, but more precisely the World Champion's main competitor for first place!

**R. Praggnanandhaa**
**Magnus Carlsen**
Miami FTX Crypto Cup 2022 (7.6)

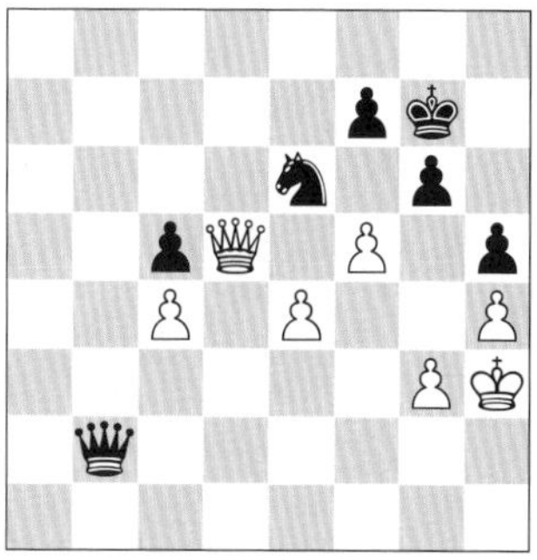

position after 47.f5

The Indian chess boom is an amazing thing to observe. I started working with Vishy Anand 20 years ago, and when I witness the long-term results of his victories in his home city and the popularity of chess there, my joy and pride at seeing this cannot be spoiled by a FIDE election. When asked to mention the names of a few outstanding Indian talents – which would be quite possible – I prefer to stick to the phrase 'no one mentioned, no one forgotten', as it fits the boom perfectly well. It's the numbers that impress – plus the fact that India can field three teams competing for medals, with the actual second team getting on the podium! Soon we will see the new generation getting invites to top tournaments, but already we get to enjoy their abilities in online chess. If Praggnanandhaa was seen as a 'talent' when he was invited to the Meltwater Champions Tour, he proved that label wrong. Talent, surely, but more precisely the World Champion's main competitor for first place! Magnus did clinch the FTX Crypto Cup, as he needed only not to lose their mini-match on the final day. But once Magnus had ensured this with a 2-1 lead (from four rapid games), the young Indian took over and won the next three games!

The final tie-break game saw Magnus needing a win to force an Armageddon, and this is where he got his chance!

**47...♕a1**

A logical move, and still winning, but 47...g5!! strikes me as both unusual and beautiful. The threat is 48... g4, mate, to which there is no reasonable reply, since taking the pawn, 48.hxg5 also leads to mate: 48...♘xg5+ 49.♔h4 ♕h2+ 50.♔xg5 f6+ 51.♔f4 ♕f2, mate.

**48.♔g2 gxf5 49.exf5 ♕b2+ 50.♔h3 ♕c1??**

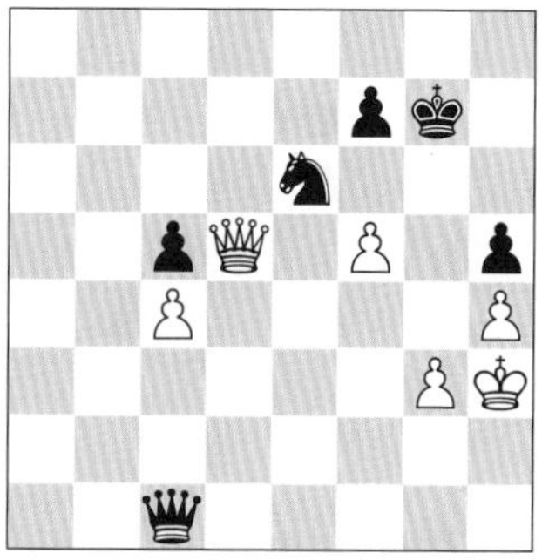

A hallucination. Zig-zagging the queen closer to the centre might look reasonable, but Magnus has forgotten that h1 is protected, so White can just take the e6-knight!

**51.fxe6 fxe6 52.♕e5+**

Here Magnus resigned, with a smile. ■

**Meltwater Champions Chess Tour 2022**

| | | A | B | C | D | E | F | |
|---|---|---|---|---|---|---|---|---|
| 1 | Magnus Carlsen | 31¼ | 32¼ | 30 | 13 | | 40 | 146½ |
| 2 | Jan-Krzysztof Duda | 4¼ | 20¾ | 35 | | 13 | 27½ | 100½ |
| 3 | R Praggnanandhaa | 4¾ | 5¼ | 30 | 21¼ | | 37½ | 98¾ |
| 4 | Le Quang Liem | 7½ | 14 | 32½ | | | 30 | 84 |
| 5 | Anish Giri | 5¼ | | 22½ | 13¼ | 8 | 17½ | 66½ |
| 6 | Levon Aronian | 5¼ | | | | 30½ | 20 | 55¾ |
| 7 | Ding Liren | 7½ | 11¾ | | 31¼ | | | 50½ |
| 8 | Shakhriyar Mamedyarov | 4¼ | | 27½ | 7½ | 4½ | | 43¾ |
| 9 | Jorden van Foreest | | 8¾ | 25 | 4¼ | | | 38 |
| 10 | Alireza Firouzja | | | | | | 37½ | 37½ |
| 11 | Wei Yi | | | | 8 | 19¾ | | 27¾ |
| 12 | Eric Hansen | 7¾ | 4 | 7½ | 3¾ | | | 23 |
| 13 | Ian Nepomniachtchi | 22¼ | | | | | | 22¼ |
| 14 | Richard Rapport | | 5¼ | | | 12¾ | | 18 |
| 15 | David Anton | | 8 | | 7 | | | 15 |
| 16 | Hans Niemann | 3¾ | 7½ | | | 3½ | 0 | 14¾ |
| 17 | Andrey Esipenko | 12 | | | | | | 12 |
| | Vladislav Artemiev | 12 | | | | | | 12 |
| 19 | Aryan Tari | | | | 7 | 4½ | | 11½ |
| 20 | Samuel Sevian | | | | | 10 | | 10 |
| 21 | Arjun Erigaisi | | | | | 9¾ | | 9¾ |
| 22 | Vidit Gujrathi | | 5 | | 4¼ | | | 9¼ |
| 23 | Pentala Harikrishna | | 4 | | 4½ | | | 8½ |
| 24 | Jeffery Xiong | | | | | 8 | | 8 |
| 25 | Vincent Keymer | 7½ | | | | | | 7½ |
| 26 | David Navara | | 7¼ | | | | | 7¼ |
| | Sam Shankland | | | | 4 | 3¼ | | 7¼ |
| 28 | Ju Wenjun | | 2½ | | | 4 | | 6½ |
| 29 | Gawain Jones | | 2½ | | 3 | | | 5½ |
| 30 | Nodirbek Abdusattorov | 4¾ | | | | | | 4¾ |
| 31 | Radosław Wojtaszek | | | | | 4½ | | 4½ |
| 32 | Leinier Domínguez | | | | | 4¼ | | 4¼ |
| 33 | Nils Grandelius | | | | 4 | | | 4 |
| 34 | Abhimanyu Mishra | | | | 2½ | | | 2½ |
| 35 | Alexandra Kosteniuk | ¾ | | | | | | ¾ |
| 36 | Lei Tingjie | | ½ | | | | | ½ |
| 37 | Teimour Radjabov | | | | | 0 | | 0 |

A = Airthings Masters; B = Charity Cup; C = Oslo Esports Cup; D = Chessable Masters; E = FTX Road to Miami; F = Miami FTX Crypto Cup

# MAXIMize your Tactics

## with Maxim Notkin

## Find the best move in the positions below

Solutions on page 87

1. Black to move

2. Black to move

3. White to move

4. White to move

5. White to move

6. Black to move

7. White to move

8. White to move

9. Black to move

# Gibraltar
## the home of
# Women's
## chess

# BEDWETTING, THE PATZER'S OPENING, AND OTHER ADVENTURES IN ADULT IMPROVEMENT

I wet the bed until I was 12 years old. Every night I'd go to bed praying, PRAYING, that 'tonight's the night I stop peeing all night while I sleep.'

Then in the morning I'd wake up – the sheets, the bed, my pajamas, my skin, totally soaked.

If I had time, I'd shower and then go to school. Sometimes I didn't have time and I'd go to school smelling of urine. I had lots of friends.

I didn't stop wetting the bed by looking at pictures of little boys sleeping with captions that said, 'little boy to move and not wet the bed'. (Actually, a book like that would be creepy).

My grandmother started waking me up at two in the morning and making sure I'd go to the bathroom.

I had to PRACTICE 'not wetting the bed' by actually doing it. Not watching videos about it (again... creepy).

Wait. Wait... this is about chess. The situation I just described is exactly why GMs say, 'Don't just study openings!' Understand the ideas, they say. But how?

A few weeks ago I was in a tournament playing a 2200+. We were playing a Sämisch King's Indian. I had studied the course. Read the books. Watched the videos. Memorized the theory.

For the first 14 moves there is not a computer on this planet that could've played better than me. I was

## I had to PRACTICE 'not wetting the bed' by actually doing it. Not watching videos about it

PERFECT. I was 99.999% accurate. I was AlphaJames.

And then on move 15 I wondered, 'Wait. What if he plays the obvious f4!?'

I tried to remember, 'Did the course mention f4 here?' I couldn't remember. (It didn't). I had no idea what I would do. 'Please don't play f4. Please don't play f4', I was thinking.

But you and I know this to be true: two chess players playing each other over the board can sometimes read each other's minds.

He played f4.

I had no idea what to do. It was like I was in the show 'Survivor', dropped off naked in the middle of the jungle and had no idea how to kill lions.

I retreated my knight, which a move earlier I had JUST moved to h5. Later the computer said that at this point I was barely over the level of functional idiot. I wasn't perfect anymore.

I went over the game with GM Jesse Kraai. He said, 'Yeah, f4 is probably not in the course because it's a very bad move!'

And we analyzed and sparred some games looking at the correct ...♗d4! instead of my retreat.

I didn't fully appreciate that in this opening, in exchange for less space I had better development and he had some loose pieces lying around.

'Study the ideas! Study the ideas!' everyone says.

I am afflicted with a giant case of Dunning-Krueger Bias (the cognitive bias that makes humans delusional about their own greatness). I assume if I know the lines I'll figure out the ideas.

During my 25-year break from tournament play I got obsessed with many things.

One year, every night I played poker. For many years I day traded. For six years I performed stand-up comedy every night on stage, seven nights a week.

Every night I went on stage was probably the equivalent of watching 40 stand-up comedy specials on Netflix in terms of learning.

I'd get home and watch the video I took of my performance from 20 minutes earlier. I'd watch it again and again.

Maybe I stuttered at the 50-second point. Or I was a little too slow with the punchline. I didn't stop and make fun of the guy in the front row who was looking at his phone. Or I looked like I had done this joke a 1000 times before instead of seeming like I was just riffing.

A thousand things I'd notice watching my bad performances. And then I'd go up the next night and repeat the process.

The learning difference between DOING (and then analysing what you DID) and simply STUDYING (without doing) is enormous.

What are we doing when we play a game of chess? We are thinking and calculating, not passively watching a video.

I go through lots of games in books or in videos. Afterwards, 'That was a great game. He really made use of that e5-square.' Or, 'Amazing queen sacrifice!'

When I go through games in a book, I like to go over as many games as possible. So I skip the thinking.

Everyone I talk to says, 'Study each game on a real board. Study each move like it's, "you to play and move" and act like it's a real game.'

In a game, what are you doing? You are calculating. So to get better at thinking and calculating you have to practice... thinking and calculating! That's all.

I had to practice getting up at 2 am every night and going to the bathroom.

And you can read books on positional play. But positional play is just a way to use well-trodden shortcuts to know what tactics the position is asking for. You still have to practice DOING positional play and not just reading about it.

The position above was begging me, 'James! Of course ...♗d4! He's barely developed and his pieces are hanging!

Why are you so stupid! Stupid!'

Incidentally, I also have a problem with too much negative self-talk in a game.

I am trying to work on that. There's no book called, 'White to move and stop calling himself an idiot after he blunders a pawn'.

Interesting statistic that explains some of the differences between a grandmaster and everyone else.

## The learning difference between DOING (and then analyzing what you DID) and simply STUDYING (without doing) is enormous

After the moves 1.e4 e5 2.♗c4 ♘c6, the move 3.♕h5?! is sometimes called the Patzer's Opening. Elite and snobbish players make fun of people who make this move, going so directly for mate.

The computers will laugh at you as well.

'-0.4' after ♕h5.

Stockfish even said to me, 'Let me get this straight: you are on move 3, you moved first, and you're already down the equivalent of half a pawn! Hahahahaha!'

Shut up, Stockfish.

Because ♕h5! is the BEST move, a 1600-rated player should play it if they want to win and they are playing another 1600-rated player.

According to the Lichess database, White (among just 1600s in the database) wins 56% of the time with this. It's the best of all the options. The computer-suggested move (the pathetically slow, 'd3???') wins only 49% of the time.

However, when I look at the database for 2500s, they win only 51% of the time with ♕h5.

Why? Because the 2500s understand why this is not a good move. Why it exposes the queen too much and the attack is trivial to repel.

I am not saying ♕h5 is a great move. But the computer and GM recommended lines have zero value (or even negative value) if you memorize them without understanding them. That includes all 27,000 books written by GMs about their favourite openings.

And yes, I know this is a cliché of what chess coaches say. But the only way I've improved since returning to tournaments is by specifically doing this:

The only way to learn the ideas, after you've watched all the videos and read the courses, is PLAYING games and then going over them.

Whether it's over-the-board play and then analysing the positions afterwards with a coach (thank you GM Jesse Kraai and, 25 years earlier, GM John Fedorowicz), blitz play online (and then reviewing them afterwards and even sparring from the critical positions), or simulating as close as possible the act of playing a game while you are studying one.

I am afraid what might be slowing down my comeback after 25 years of no play might not be tactics or positional play or bad endgame knowledge.

It might be laziness (and negative self-talk).

I like quantity over quality. It's hard to set up each game and think about each move as if I were in a real game. It's hard to analyse EVERY blitz game. Particularly on those all-night obsessive sessions.

But when I started doing this analysis (or I should say, 'started doing it more than zero') I saw my online ratings go up several hundred points. My low on Lichess rapid was 1799 over a year ago and now it's 2400.

And I started bouncing off my lows in real over-the-board games.

The first few tournaments after 25 years of no play I dropped an instant two hundred rating points. I would cry on the plane home. I was ashamed to face my children after each tournament..

Because despite what our psychiatrists tell us, chess rating is indeed equivalent to self-worth. And no anti-depressant medications will change that.

The past few months I've bounced about 100 points after taking reviewing my games more seriously. And doing lots more tactical puzzles (again: practicing at home what I do over the board – thinking).

Even reviewing my blitz games. And setting up Kaspa-rov's games on the board and pausing after each move (well, almost every move. Or every fifth move. I need to do this better).

And sparring from critical positions in my openings rather than just memorizing them. Oh, and playing ♕h5 more against lower-rated players.

But there are also other problems I have that are just as important.

I've spoken to sports psychologists, chess coaches, and even neurologists about my negative self-talk in the middle of a game.

Once I start losing it's hard to generate counterplay when a voice in my head is constantly whispering, 'loser'.

There's a scene in the TV series *Mad Men* where the character Mike Ginsberg says to Don Draper, 'I think you're a very sad man.'

And Don Draper says, as he is walking away towards another successful day, 'That's funny, I don't think about you at all.'

I need to be like that. And maybe I've started making some progress. At least I don't wet the bed after a bad tournament.

■ ■ ■

By the way, a few moves later in my game with the 2200-rated player mentioned above,

Black to move and get a significant advantage. I ended up winning the game.

(Solution: knight to g four.)

James Altucher has written 25 books. About 21 of them are bad but one or two are OK. He has started several companies and has a popular podcast called 'The James Altucher Show'. Among others, Garry Kasparov and Judit Polgar have been guests on his podcast, as well as Kareem Abdul-Jabbar, Richard Branson and 963 others. He has played chess since he was 16 but stopped when he hit 2204 USCF in 1997, and is now starting to play again.

Thomas Willemze

# What would you play?

Opposite-coloured bishops are often associated with drawish tendencies. That's not always true. They can be fierce attackers.

**S**ome people tend to avoid positions with opposite-coloured bishops because they fear their drawish reputation in an eventual ending. This is unfortunate, because they will miss out a lot of fun in the middlegame! Opposite-coloured bishops can be very dynamic and a dangerous weapon in case of an attack on the enemy king.

## Exercises

**Pawel Kossowski** (1737) and **Tymoteusz Bem** (1682) played a game that was everything but drawish in the 2022 Baltic Pearl Open in the holiday resort Lazy in Poland.

I created four exercises in which you can experience the complexity of opposite-coloured bishops yourself.

## Exercise 1

position after 19...♔f8

The black pawn made it all the way to a3 and threatens to capture on b2. How would you respond? Capture the attacker with **20.bxa3**, protect the b2-pawn with **20.0-0-0**, or bolster the dark squares with **20.b4** ?

## Exercise 2

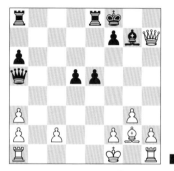

position after 22.♗g2

Black successfully set his d-pawn into motion and has a very pleasant position. How should he continue? Immediately block the white bishop with **22...e4**, develop the rook with **22...♖ad8**, or continue aggressively with **22...♕d2** ?

## Exercise 3

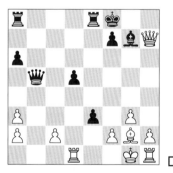

position after 24...e3

This position could have occurred in the game if Black would have pushed his pawn to e3. Should White capture the pawn with **25.fxe3**, or ignore it with **25.♗f3** ?

## Exercise 4

position after 25...♕d2

How should White improve his position? Pull back the queen with **26.♕h5**, break the centre with **26.c4**, or push the h-pawn with **26.h4** ?

I hope you enjoyed these exercises and managed to benefit from the unbalanced nature of the position. You can find the full analysis of this game on the next pages.

**Opposite-coloured bishops can be very dynamic and a dangerous weapon in case of an attack on the enemy king**

**Pawel Kossowski** (1737)
**Tymoteusz Bem** (1682)
Lazy 2022
Sicilian Defence, Sveshnikov Variation

**1.e4 c5 2.♘f3 ♘c6 3.d4 cxd4
4.♘xd4 ♘f6 5.♘c3 e5 6.♘db5 d6
7.♗g5 a6 8.♘a3 b5**

**9.♗xf6 gxf6**
Recapturing with the pawn is very typical in the Sveshnikov. 9...♕xf6 looks like a decent alternative, but runs into a thematic piece sacrifice after 10.♘d5 ♕d8:

**ANALYSIS DIAGRAM**

11.♗xb5! axb5 12.♘xb5. Black is in trouble, because the upcoming 13.

♘bc7+ is either a double attack, or results in mate after 13...♔d7 14. ♕g4+ f5 15.♕xf5. The only way to parry both threats seems 12...♕a5+ 13.c3 ♖b8, but the black queen runs out of options after 14.b4!.
**10.♘d5 ♗g7 11.g3**

**11...f5**
Black trades the newly created f-pawn to soften his opponent's grip on the d5-square.
**12.exf5 ♗xf5 13.♗g2 0-0
14.♘e3 ♘e7**

**15.♘xf5**
Picking up the exchange with 15.♗xa8 was possible, but certainly

not without risk. Black gets decent compensation after 15...♕xa8 16.0-0 ♗e6 17.♖xd6 ♘c6.
**15...♘xf5 16.♕h5**

From now on, the **opposite-coloured bishops** will have a profound influence on the course of the game.
**16...b4**
Black trades his active knight for White's passive one on the rim. 16...♘d4 would therefore have been the better choice.
**17.♕xf5 bxa3 18.♗e4 ♖e8
19.♕xh7+ ♔f8**

**20.bxa3**
This move goes at the expense of White's castling rights and enables

Black to set his centre into motion. The right answer to **Exercise 1** was 20.b4!.

ANALYSIS DIAGRAM

White needs this pawn on the dark squares to complement the light-squared bishop! Black can still push his d-pawn with 20...d5, but White can block it with 21.♖d1! d4 22.♖d3 and get an overwhelming advantage. 20.0-0-0 is not a bad move, but leads to unnecessary counterplay after 20...♖b8!.

**20...♕a5+ 21.♔f1 d5 22.♗g2**

We have arrived at **Exercise 2**.

**22...e4!**

Well played! Black needs his pawns on the light squares to free his bishop and restrict the white counterpart. 22...♖ad8 looks very natural, but the rook should rather go to c8 in the future, to attack the c2-pawn. 22...♕d2 is the least attractive option and gives White a pleasant position after 23.♕d3! ♕xd3+ 24.cxd3 e4 25.♖d1!.

**23.♖d1 ♕b5+**

The simple 23...♖ac8 looks even stronger.

**24.♔g1**

nothing wrong with 25.♖xd5! ♖ad8 26.♖xd8 ♖xd8 27.h4!.

**25...♕d2** A move like 25...♖ac8 would again have secured a serious advantage for Black. The text move is too slow and brings us to **Exercise 4**.

**24...♕e2** This move unnecessarily sacrifices the d5-pawn. 24...♖e5 and 24...♖ac8 would have preserved Black's large advantage.
24...e3 is worse and leads to **Exercise 3**.

ANALYSIS DIAGRAM

This position might look scary for White and he would indeed end up in trouble after 25.fxe3 ♖xe3 26.♖f1 ♕b6!.
The key is to create a safe spot for the king on the light squares with 25.♗f3!.

ANALYSIS DIAGRAM

This move vacates the g2-square for the king. White is totally fine after 25...e2 26.♖e1 ♖ac8 27.♔g2 and even better after 25...exf2+ 26.♔g2 ♖ad8 27.♖hf1, followed by 28.♖xf2.

**25.♖f1** Too passive. There was

**26.♕h5** This clever move worked very well, but is objectively not sound. 26.c4 is also ill-advised, on account of 26...e3! 27.fxe3 ♕xe3+ 28.♔f2 ♖e6, followed by 29...♖f6. Instead, White should focus on releasing his worst placed piece and opt for 26.h4!.

ANALYSIS DIAGRAM

A dynamic balance arises after 26...♖ac8 27.h5 ♖xc2 28.h6 ♗d4.

ANALYSIS DIAGRAM

29.♖h4 ♗xf2+ 30.♔h1.

**26...e3**

This is exactly what White was hoping for. 26...♖ac8 would have kept Black in full control.

**27.♗xd5!** This in-between move threatens 28.♕xf7 mate and suddenly turns the tables.

**27...♖a7**

**28.fxe3!**

This time, White does not mind capturing the pawn because his king will be safe on g2 and he can quickly develop pressure along the open f-file.

**28...♕xe3+ 29.♔g2!**

The white king is completely safe on the light squares, whereas Black has the impossible task to withstand the pressure on his f7-pawn.

---

**29...♖ee7 30.♖f2 ♕d4 31.♖hf1**

Black clearly starts to feel that he is a full piece down on the light squares.

**31...♖e5** This is the most practical attempt, since 31...f6 32.♖xf6+ ♗xf6 33.♕h8 is mate!

# Picking different colours for your bishop and pawns eases the movement of your own bishop, while restricting the enemy counterpart

**32.♖xf7+ ♔e8 33.♖f8+ ♔d7 34.♕f7+ ♖e7**

**35.♕f5+!**

White uses the light squares to chase the enemy king to the other side of the board.

---

**35...♔d6 36.♖d8+ ♔c7 37.♖c8+ ♔b6**

There was no way back, because 37...♔d6 38.♖c6 is mate.

**38.♖b1+ ♔a5 39.♗e6+ ♗e5**

**40.♖e1**

White attacks the pinned piece and forces his opponent to surrender an exchange.

**40...♖xe6 41.♕xe6 ♕d2+ 42.♔f1 ♗c7**

**43.♕c4**

43.♖e5+ ♗xe5 44.♖c5+ ♔a4 45.♕b3 mate would have been the quickest win, but the text move leads to the same result.

**43...♔d6 44.♖c5+ ♔b6 45.♖b1+** Black resigned.

**Conclusion**

This game demonstrated that positions with opposite-coloured bishops can be highly dynamical, with a crucial role to the safety of the kings.

An important technique to remember is to pick different colours for your bishop and your pawns. This will ease the movement of your own bishop, while restricting the enemy counterpart as much as possible. ∎

# MAXIMize your Tactics Solutions

**1. Siva-Bodnaruk**
Titled Tuesday 2022

**45...♘g3+!** By sacrificing the knight, Black opens up both the f-file and the 5th rank. **46.hxg3 ♖f1+ 47.♖xf1 ♖xf1+ 48.♔h2 ♛h5** Mate.

**2. Manish -Iniyan**
Guwahati 2022

After **17...♛xd4!** White played **18.♛f3**, wisely avoiding 18.♛xd4 ♘g3+ 19.♔g1 ♘e2+ and 20...♘xd4, but of course this lost too.

**3. Gunina-Plazuelo**
Titled Tuesday 2022

**36.♖xf6!** Black resigned, as he loses the queen after both 36...♔xf6 37.♗e3+ and 36...♛xf6 37.♗h6+.

**4. Donchenko-Can**
Fagernes 2022

**20.♖xe6+!** ♔xe6 20...♔f8 21.♛xd7 ♛xh5 22.♖xd4 is absolutely hopeless. **21.♖e1+ ♔f5 22.♛a5+!** Perhaps Black reckoned with 22.♛xd7+ ♔g5 only. Now he resigned in view of 22...♔f4 23.g3+.

**5. Sarana-Abdyjapar**
Titled Tuesday 2022

**30.♖h7! ♛xc5** The king can't run: 30...♔xe7 31.♖gxg7+ ♔f8 (31...♔d8 32.♖xd7+; 31...♔f6 32.♛e3) 32.♖xd7!. **31.♖gxg7+ ♔e8** If 31...♔f6 32.♖g6 or 32.♘g8! mate. **32.♖g8** Mate.

**6. Sadhwani-Williams**
Reykjavik 2022

**32...♘g5!** Threatening 33...♘h3+. **33.f3** (33.hxg5 ♛h5 at once is similar) **33...gxf3 34.hxg5 ♛h5** White resigned. The desperate 35.♖g7+ ♔xg7 36.gxf6+ ♔xf6 and so on doesn't help to prevent ...♛h1+.

**7. Bluebaum-Giri**
Chess.com 2022

**28.♘xf7!** More human than 28.♘xe6+! ♛xe6 (28...fxe6 29.♖xd7 ♛xg3 30.fxg3+) 29.♗xd7 ♖xd7 when White should see 30.♛c3!. **28...♛xg3** If 28...♔xf7 29.♖xd7+ wins material. **29.fxg3!** and White went on to win.

**8. Gurel-Pastar**
Ayvalik 2022

**44.♗xe5!** ♔xe5 44...hxg2 45.♗h2 stopping the pawn. **45.♘e1 ♔f4 46.♘f3!! ♔xf3 47.a6 h2 48.a7 ♔f2 49.a8♛ ♔g1 50.♛a1+ ♔g2 51.♛xg7** 51...h1♛ 52.♛b7+, with decisive liquidation. Black resigned.

**9. Sadhwani-Sarana**
Titled Tuesday 2022

**33...♛e4+ 34.♔h3** On 34.♔f1, Black mates in two. **34...g5! 35.♛xc5** Avoiding 35...g4+ 36.♔h4 ♗e7+, but Black has other attacking ideas. **35...g4+ 36.♔h4 g5+ 37.♔xg5 ♛f5+ 38.♔h4 ♔g7** Mate is inevitable, White resigned.

Judit Polgar

# Chances for everyone

There is no chess event that exemplifies FIDE's motto *Gens Una Sumus* better than the Olympiad. Commentating for the official broadcast from Chennai, **JUDIT POLGAR** had a first-hand view of the action and had particular pleasure watching lower-rated players upsetting favourites.

**T**he Olympiad is a unique chess event that connects players from different continents and cultures – a true festival that brings together amateurs and top professionals, including the World Champion. Top players aim at winning medals, but also look forward to meeting old friends. The strongest teams start out with the hope of obtaining an honourable place, while the many others are delighted to play alongside their idols. Talking about variety, it is worth mentioning that in Chennai the youngest participant was eight years old and the oldest 76!

The All India Chess Federation had barely four months to organize the Olympiad in Chennai, but they coped with the job marvellously. I was impressed by the immense number of volunteers involved in the organization, most of them chess enthusiasts. They obviously appreciated the opportunity of being around great players, were knowledgeable and very helpful and... frequently asked me to give autographs or take selfies with them. I must confess that sometimes I had to take the back road to reach the playing hall without delay, trying to escape the pleasant

but time-consuming autograph and selfies sessions...

On one occasion, a fan approached me to share the analysis he had done on an endgame played there. I immediately noticed that he was really good and very fast!

The first time I took part in a Chess Olympiad, in Thessaloniki 1988, I was a 12-year-old prodigy, scoring 12½ out of 13 and winning gold for Hungary together with my sisters and Ildiko Madl. Two years later, we repeated this feat. I remember that in those years, I enjoyed the attention of the media and the chess fans in a similar way as Gukesh did in Chennai.

Starting from 1994, I have participated in the open section and collected two team silver medals, which I treasure as much as I treasure the gold ones.

When they start, Olympiads are like empty pages waiting to be filled with surprises. Talented youngsters have

an excellent opportunity to make the news, but irrespective of age, strongly motivated teams can prove that clear rating differences do not necessarily count when sitting down at the table.

Chennai 2022 was no exception. The young teams of Uzbekistan (with an average age of 20.4 years) and India 2 (19.6 years) were among the protagonists fighting for the gold medals throughout the tournament. At the same time, the formidable USA team, enjoying a huge rating advantage over the other favourites, did not seem 'hungry enough' for a win and became a shadow of what their fans might have hoped they would be.

### Discipline and focus

I have always been of the classical opinion (some may call it old-fashioned) that discipline and focus are essential for achieving results, even more so than rating and experience. From this point of view, the following

**Strongly motivated teams can prove that clear rating differences do not necessarily count when sitting down at the table**

story about Ivan Sokolov, the captain of the Uzbeki team, is relevant. Asked by his players whether he would allow them to attend the traditional Bermuda Party, Ivan answered with a categorical 'No!' He added that, in order to prevent the young players from feeling that he had betrayed them, he would – for the first time since 1988 – refrain from going to the party as well.

However, I can also understand that there is no universal recipe for success. In an interview given after the Olympiad, the USA woman player Tatev Abrahamyan confessed that her team played much better during the final five rounds after... going to the Bermuda Party! It seems that the term 'discipline' can have a wide meaning, and can also refer to one's ability of knowing what suits one best.

## Upsets and surprises

Leaving these abstract thoughts aside, I will examine a few examples of games convincingly won by the lower-rated player. My aim is to highlight the fact that at Olympiads, games are not won by simply proving a higher rating, or a more impressive visiting card than your opponent.

One of the greatest early surprises was seen in Round 2, when Zambia (average rating 2314) defeated Denmark (2566). The games on the first three boards ended in draws (although the final position on the top board was completely winning for the Zambian player), and the match was decided by this game.

**Nase Lungu (2216)**
**Martin Haubro (2411)**
Chennai Olympiad 2022 (2)

position after 26...♘b7

White has a slight advantage due to his centralized rook and Black's doubled pawns. With his next two moves, Lungu shows that he understands the importance of global centralization.
**27.♕d3! g6 28.♕d4**
Apart from dominating the centre, White is threatening the deadly ♘g4.
**28...h5 29.h3 ♖e6**

**30.g4!** White's systematic play impressed me deeply, even though some of his concrete moves were not the strongest. The latter does not apply to the last move, by the way.
**30...hxg4 31.hxg4**
Aiming for g4-g5 and ♘g4.
31.♘xg4 was an important alterna-

tive: 31...♖xe2 32.♘h6+ ♔f8 33.♕h8+ ♔e7 34.♘g8+, with a strong attack.

**31...♖d6?!**
Black wrongly identifies his target. It was essential to fight against the centralized queen with 31...♕b6 32.♕f4 ♕c6, when White keeps a small plus.
**32.g5 ♖xd5?** Only helping White to speed up his attack.
**33.♘xd5 ♕c1+ 34.♔h2 ♕c5** Too late. **35.♘f6+ ♔g7 36.♕h4**

**36...♕d6+** As we will see, the queen will block the king's escape on this square, but due to a series of geometrical ideas Black does not have a satisfactory defence against ♕h6 mate.
36...♔f8 would run into 37.♘d7+, winning the queen.
36...♕c7+ 37.f4 ♔f8 loses to 38.♘d5!, attacking the queen and threatening ♕h8 mate.
**37.f4 ♔f8 38.♕h8+ ♔e7 39.♕e8** Mate.

The greatest upset of the Open Olympiad was the performance and final result (59th place) of the third seed, Norway, with a rating average of 2692. True, their high position

Zambia upset much higher rated Denmark thanks to Nase Lungu's win on Board 4.

in the initial ranking was largely due to Magnus Carlsen's 'cosmic rating', but even if he had had, say, a hundred points less, Norway would still have started as the 7th seed.

It was inspiring to see Magnus playing all the games between Rounds 2 and 10, but it seems that for the other team members the pressure of being among the favourites was too high. However, I believe that at the next Olympiad, which will take place in my hometown of Budapest in 2024, they will become real contenders for the medals.

The equal score of 2-2 against the much lower rated (2478) team of Mongolia in Round 4 showed that Carlsen's excellent play was not enough for an overall good result. The World Champion won, but Mongolia levelled the score on Board 4.

**Sugar Gan-Erdene** (2428)
**Frode Olav Olsen Urkedal** (2555)
Chennai Olympiad 2022 (4)

position after 9...a5

In this type of position, White usually faces problems developing his queen's knight. ♘c3 usually runs into ...dxc4, while after b2-b3, Black can continue with ...b7-b6 and ...♗a6, renewing White's problems.
**10.♘bd2** This blocks the bishop's retreat to c1 and is supposed to cause White some discomfort. However, the 19-year-old Mongolian displays a refined understanding of the system and maintains the fluency of his play.
**10...♘h5 11.♗e3 f5 12.♘b3!** Not only clearing the bishop's retreat to d2, but also preparing the knight's transfer closer to e5.

**12...♗d6 13.♘c1**

**13...b5** Trying to catch up in development, but creating a new weakness on c5. With his queenside underdeveloped, Black would not get much out of early kingside aggression: 13...f4 14.♗d2 g5 15.♘d3 g4?! 16.♘fe5, with a large advantage for White.
**14.cxb5 cxb5 15.♕c6 ♘b6 16.♘d3**

Completing the first part of White's manoeuvre and preparing to increase his control over the c-file.
**16...♕d7 17.♕xd7 ♗xd7 18.♘fe5 ♖fd8 19.b3 ♗a3 20.♗c1 ♗d6 21.♘c5**

Now that the white knights have occupied the weak squares, White has a huge positional advantage.

**21...♗c8 22.♗d2 ♖e8 23.♖fc1 ♘f6 24.♘c6 a4 25.♗f4 ♗f8 26.e3 ♘fd7 27.♗c7** In view of the threat of ♗f1 (with or without a previous exchange on b6), Black has problems keeping his queenside intact.

**27...b4** This gives up a pawn without any compensation, but 27...♘xc5 28.dxc5 ♘d7 29.b4 ♗a6 30.♘d4 does not offer too much hope either.
**28.♗xb6 ♘xb6 29.♘xb4 ♗d7 30.♗f1** White won on move 59.

Apart from the young medallists, the most pleasant surprise of the open section was provided by Moldova. Seeded 48th, with a rating average of 2462, they finished 6th. In the last three rounds, Moldova defeated Romania, Norway and England.

Here is their last-round win on Board 2, which sealed their match victory and a fantastic final result.

**Luke McShane** (2649)
**Vladimir Hamitevici** (2473)
Chennai Olympiad 2022 (11)

position after 36...g4

White is a pawn up and Black's position might seem a bit overextended. However, the vulnerability of the h4-pawn makes things unclear.

**37.♖de2?!** This yields Black easy play. Without ensuring an advantage, 37.♖f2 would have been more challenging: 37...d3! (the same pawn break as later in the game, clearing the d4-square for the queen. Unlike in the game, 37... gxf3? is bad due to 38.♖xf3!, when Black's kingside becomes vulnerable) 38.cxd3 ♕d4 39.♘e3 (unpinning the f3-pawn) 39...♖f4 (threatening to win the h4-pawn with ...gxf3) 40.fxg4 hxg4 41.♘d1 ♘h5 42.♕e3 g3, and after retrieving the pawn on h4, Black will have good compensation for his slight material deficit.

**37...gxf3! 38.gxf3** In the event of 38.♕g6, Black can defend his rook with 38...e4!, leading to unclear play.

**38...♖g8 39.♕h3 e4!** A well-timed pawn sacrifice, neutralizing White's pressure along the e-file. **40.fxe4 ♖f4!**

Moldova's Vladimir Hamitevici (2473) was in great shape with a 2604 performance on Board 3.

**41.♖f1?** The only way to stay in the game was 41.♕h2!. **41...d3!** A second pawn break, clearing the g1-a7 diagonal for the queen.

**42.♖e3** The point behind the last pawn sacrifice is that 42.cxd3 would run into 42...♖g3! 43.♕xg3 ♖xf1+,

winning, e.g. 44.♔h2 (44.♔g2 ♖g1+ is no better) 44...♘g4+ 45.♔h3 ♖h1+ 46.♔g2 ♖g1+.

**42...dxc2 43.♖xf4** A desperate attempt to change things. In the event of 43.♖c1 ♘xe4, Black's attack will be decisive.

**43...c1♕+ 44.♖f1 ♕c2 45.♖xf6**

Did White finally get some activity? **45...♕xe4+!** Not really! This pseudo-sacrifice maintains the decisive initiative.

**46.♖ff3** 46.♖xe4 ♕g1 mate.

**46...♕cd4** The material balance is reasonable for White, but his king is hopelessly exposed. Engines announce mate in eight, but Hami-

tevici won a bit more slowly, with 'boring' human moves.

**47.♕f1 ♕c2** The quickest mate arises after 47...♕xh4+ 48.♖h3 ♕d5+ 49.♔h2 (49.♖ef3 loses to 49...♕xf3+ 50.♕xf3 ♕e1+) 49...♕f4+!, overloading the white queen and mating soon. **48.♘e5 ♕db2!**

The only winning move, but an obvious one, surely planned one move earlier.

**49.♘f7+ ♔h7 50.♘g5+ ♖xg5!** The rest is agony.

**51.♖f7+ ♖g7 52.♖e2 ♕c6+** 52...♕xe2 53.♕f5+ ♔h8 54.♖f8+ ♖g8 also wins, but for practical reasons it is wiser to attack with checks.

**53.♔h2 ♕d6+ 54.♔h1 ♕d5+ 55.♖f3 ♕f6 56.♖ef2 ♕xh4+ 57.♖h2 ♕xf3+! 58.♕xf3 ♕e1+ 59.♕f1 ♕xf1** Mate.

## Conclusions:

■ Ambition, focus and discipline are key ingredients of success

■ One should not be inhibited by one's opponent's higher rating.

■ Every player should know his or her optimal tournament regime. ■

# Openings Everywhere

As he was following the engine world championships and musing about Magnus Carlsen's decision not to defend his title, **MATTHEW SADLER** was inevitably thinking about openings a lot. Fortunately, there was a fine selection of new opening books waiting to be savoured and enjoyed.

**M**y chess life in the past couple of weeks has been dominated by World Championships. I was following the various engine world championships (3 events: software, computer and speed) in Vienna run by the ICGA (International Computer Games Association), and pondering Magnus Carlsen's recent confirmation that he would not defend his title in the next World Championship match. Funnily enough, the first got me thinking about the second!

Unlike at the TCEC or chess.com (where unbalanced openings are pre-selected for engine games to ensure decisive results and entertainment) the games at the ICGA championships started from the standard opening position, and engines were allowed access to an opening book of their choosing. It was noticeable how – just like in human play – signif-icant differences in strength could be bridged by a deep and well-crafted opening book. We saw numerous games where the game essentially started in a resolved situation where it was impossible for the weaker side to lose. The World Computer Chess Championship (where each engine was run on powerful(!) hardware of the entrants' choosing) ended in a tie between top engines Komodo Dragon and Leela Zero. The tie-break was four rapid games followed by an Armageddon game. Considering that a match between Komodo Dragon and Leela Zero from the starting position without book would

**The World Championship is probably the closest thing in over-the board chess to engine chess**

produce 100 draws, you can imagine that Black in the Armageddon was of crucial importance, and this time Komodo Dragon was the lucky one! However, you still have to try, and the Leela developers looked for ways to create an unusual game. I followed their conversations in Discord – and made a couple of suggestions too – and it was uncanny how similar it all sounded to last-minute human prep-aration, where you find out who you're playing an hour before the game and you desperately scrabble around for a playable, offbeat line to create winning chances!

In the end the Leela developers went with 1.h3(!) for the last regular playoff game...

**Leela Chess Zero**
**Komodo Dragon**
Vienna, World Computer Chess Championship 2022 (11.4)
Clemenz Opening

**1.h3**

**1...c5 2.e4 e6 3.♘c3 ♛b6 4.g3 ♘c6 5.a4 ♘f6 6.♗g2 d5**

And then a Fischer-style King's Indian Attack for the Armageddon:

Leela Chess Zero
Komodo Dragon
Vienna, World Computer Chess
Championship 2022 (11.5)
King's Indian Attack

**1.♘f3 d5 2.g3 c5 3.♗g2 ♘f6
4.0-0 e6 5.d3 ♘c6 6.♘bd2 ♗e7
7.e4 0-0 8.♖e1 b5 9.e5**

It didn't work, but, coupled with Komodo Dragon's sportingly aggressive play, it made for entertaining and thrilling final games! However, it's clear how difficult it is to manufacture a win from the starting position against a strong and well-prepared opponent.

Turning now to Magnus Carlsen's decision, I guess that the World Championship is probably the closest thing in over-the board chess to engine chess. The format – a long run-up period, a single opponent, vast amounts of computing resources for analysis – maximises each player's stability and puts a premium on openings. The risk of both players neutralising each other with concrete engine preparation has been high for some years already and only increases with time.

Magnus has been preparing for World Championships since 2013: he must have drawing lines worked out to 40 moves deep in every opening! I could imagine that the attraction of going through this experience continually is something that could pall over time... and not just for the players but also for spectators. At the end of the day, human frailty in the face of challenging competitive

circumstances is what keeps chess interesting as a spectator sport, and for the amazing elite players of today, you need something in the format to make it happen – whether it's the shorter time-controls we've seen in online events, a series of inbuilt competitive crises (like the sets systems that Magnus proposed, also seen in online events) or tournaments with a varied and colourful range of participants (as for example, Tata Steel always manages).

The reassuring thing, however, is that this is only a concern for the very summit of the game. Drop a few levels and there are enough mistakes, forgotten preparation and randomness to keep playing chess fascinating for us for a whole lifetime!

■ ■ ■

As you can imagine, openings have been very much on my mind and I was lucky enough to have a fine selection of opening books to occupy me this month. We start off with two books that have made the transition from Chessable course to printed book: *The Jobava System* by Simon Williams (Everyman) and *King's Kalashnikov Sicilian* by Daniel King (Chessable). On the evidence of these two books, transferring material from an online course to book form works very well indeed! Online courses are typically less variation-dense than books, as it costs too much time to demonstrate a string of sub-variations! This leads to books that seem well-suited to the needs of club players: focused on the main lines, with a limited amount of detail.

*The Jobava System* is one of those lines that would have been dismissed as amateurish in the pre-computer age but that in our more eclectic times seems just as likely to secure White an opening advantage as main line 1.d4 / 2.c4 openings! Simon Williams starts with an overview of typical ideas for inspiration, followed by a 'Quick-starter' providing an overview of the

**The Jobava System
Simon Williams
Everyman, 2022**
★★★★☆

main lines before we hit 13 chapters covering specific lines. Each chapter starts with a couple of inspirational games before we get into the specific theory of the line. Often a couple of alternatives are presented against each line: a sober continuation, and another crazier line that is clear has Simon's personal preference! One

## The Jobava System seems just as likely to secure White an opening advantage as main line 1.d4/2.c4 openings!

good example of this is the line 3...a6, which is Stockfish's preferred choice at high depths.
**1.d4 ♘f6 2.♘c3 d5 3.♗f4 a6 4.e3 e6**

Here Simon provides analysis of both the restrained **5.♗d3** and the crazy **5.g4**. Oddly enough, this variation occurred in the game between Komodo Dragon and The Baron (a venerable engine that ended up as the punching bag) at the World Computer Championship, and here

Komodo Dragon unleashed the novelty

**5.h4!** I'll give the game briefly here as it was an absolute stunner!

**5...c5 6.g4 ♕b6 7.g5 ♕xb2 8.♘ge2 ♘h5 9.♖b1 ♕a3 10.♗h2 cxd4 11.♖b3 ♕a5 12.♘xd4**

**12...g6 13.♗e2 ♘d7 14.♗xh5 gxh5 15.0-0 ♗g7 16.♘ce2 ♘c5 17.♘f4 ♘xb3 18.axb3 ♗e5 19.♗g3**

**19...♕c3 20.♘xh5 ♗xg3 21.fxg3 ♕xe3+ 22.♔g2 e5 23.♖e1 ♗g4 24.♘f6+ ♔f8 25.♘xg4 ♕xd4 26.♕f3 e4 27.♕f4 ♕b6 28.c4 ♖d8 29.♖f1 ♕e6 30.♕c7 ♕e7 31.♕b6 ♕d6 32.♕f2 ♕c7 33.♕d4 ♖g8 34.cxd5 ♖g7 35.♘f6**

AlphaZero-style domination!

**35...e3 36.♕xe3 ♕e7 37.♕d4 ♕e2+ 38.♖f2 ♕e7 39.♖f5 ♕e2+ 40.♔h3 ♕e6 41.♕b4+ ♕e7 42.♕c3 b6 43.h5 ♕b7 44.♕e5 ♕e7 45.♕d4 ♖a8 46.♖e5 ♕c5 47.♕e4 ♕c8+ 48.♔h4** 1-0

It's a very good book that I enjoyed reading through, and even without too much effort I felt I'd picked up quite a few interesting ideas in this line! Recommended. 4 stars!

■ ■ ■

*King's Kalashnikov Sicilian* by Daniel King (Chessable) is a hardback Chessable production with the same pleasant layout we saw in Judit Polgar's book (reviewed last month). The build-up is quite similar to Simon Williams's book: a first part of Model Games where King coins evocative names for some typical Kalashnikov manoeuvres such as the 'Bad-Bishop bounce' (...♗e7-d8-b6), the 'Trojan Horse' (...♘d4) and (my favourite) the 'Poke' (...♗g4). It's a nice way of stimulating readers to recognise typical themes: it certainly worked for me! The subsequent sections are theoretical sections, covering all White's possibilities quite thoroughly. I was a little surprised at first that after:

**1.e4 c5 2.♘f3 ♘c6 3.d4 cxd4 4.♘xd4 e5**

Danny gave so much coverage of White's moves 5.♘b3, 5.♘f3 and 5.♘e2 ... However, I imagine that this simply reflects the emphasis on assisting club players, as I imagine that these are more common replies to

**King's Kalashnikov Sicilian**
**Daniel King**
**Chessable, 2022**
★★★★☆

Black's unusual (at club level) system than the critical 5.♘b5. I thought that maybe lines with 6.c4 ...

**1.e4 c5 2.♘f3 ♘c6 3.d4 cxd4 4.♘xd4 e5 5.♘b5 d6 6.c4**

... might have gotten a bit more attention relatively speaking, as I think

## King coins evocative names for typical Kalashnikov manoeuvres such as the 'Bad-Bishop bounce', the 'Trojan Horse' and the 'Poke'

they are quite tricky to handle for Black (I've always found so anyway), but I guess I'll trust Danny on this one.

I had a reasonable amount of knowledge of the Kalashnikov and I certainly learnt a lot of new stuff from this book! Recommended! 4 stars!

■ ■ ■

The last pure opening book we will look at is Gawain Jones's *Coffeehouse Repertoire Volume 2* (Quality Chess). The word 'coffeehouse' conjures up images in me of something light and frivolous and carefree but that doesn't quite capture the essence of this 568-page monster! The purpose of the *Coffeehouse Repertoire* is neatly described by Gawain in his introduction: 'Primarily I wanted the choices to be sound. I've wasted too much time trying to fix holes in dodgy lines to inflict them on you. Of course these recommendations will work best if they surprise your opponent, but I believe they all have inherent merit too. Secondly, I wanted the repertoire to pack a genuine punch. Surprising your opponent with an insipid line may work occasionally, but will hardly scare a well-prepared opponent. With this repertoire, even if your opponent knows what's coming, they won't have an easy time. Thirdly, I aimed for relatively offbeat choices where possible, provided they meet the above two criteria. A lot of your opponents are unlikely to have faced these lines many times (if at all).'

The lines Gawain chooses fit these goals beautifully. My favourite and the most spectacular recommendation is definitely 5.♖g1 against the Philidor...
**1.e4 d6 2.d4 ♘f6 3.♘c3 e5 4.♘f3 ♘bd7 5.♖g1**

But the most impressive part of the book is undoubtedly the analysis of the Scotch Gambit:
**1.e4 e5 2.♘f3 ♘c6 3.♗c4 ♘f6 4.d4 exd4 5.e5**

**Coffeehouse Repertoire Volume 2**
**Gawain Jones**
**Quality Chess, 2021**
★★★★★

...and the 'Forcing Italian':
**1.e4 e5 2.♘f3 ♘c6 3.♗c4 ♗c5 4.c3 ♘f6 5.d4 exd4 6.e5**

I grew up (pre-computer age) believing that these lines were nothing at all for White (the books I read as a kid said so!) and I've never really been able to let go of that feeling despite seeing these lines played at the top level. However, you simply have to marvel at the ingenuity Jones displays in finding new and promising paths in plenty of lines I would tend to abandon as without chances.

It's really high-class modern preparation and frankly amazing to see it in a book like this! Jones also completes the whole circuit by examining different move orders in great detail (e.g. 1.e4 e5 2.d4!? exd4 3.♘f3), explaining the pros and cons clearly while providing some really interesting analysis.

It's a great book, and is warmly recommended to any player looking for something fresh in their repertoire! Wonderful stuff: 5 stars!

■ ■ ■

The final opening-related book for this month is a very interesting one: *How to Out-Prepare Your Opponent* by Jeroen Bosch (New In Chess). As the title suggests, it's not actually about specific openings (though, as befits the author of the SOS-Openings series, a lot of interesting and unusual lines are covered) but about how to approach the opening phase. It's a really interesting topic and one that is frequently misunderstood. Good openings are often reduced to nothing more than depth of knowledge and a good memory, but effective play in the opening phase has much more to it than that.

It's a serious topic, so the first chapter was a slightly surprising one: 'Tactics in the opening', detailing all manner of opening tricks into which strong players have fallen! Bosch explains the reason for this chapter as follows: 'One of the most dangerous situations arises when you lull yourself into thinking that getting a few pieces out is all you have to do at the beginning of the game and that you can start thinking concretely when the middlegame arises. It becomes even more dangerous when you think you are playing theory (but you have misremembered your lines).' One of the examples he gives is this famous opening 'oops':

## Jones displays great ingenuity in finding new and promising paths in plenty of lines that I would tend to abandon as without chances

**Loek van Wely**
**Jeroen Piket**
Tilburg 1997
English Opening, Agincourt Defence

**1.c4 e6 2.♘c3 b6 3.g3 ♗b7 4.♘f3 ♗b4 5.♗g2 ♘e7 6.♕c2 c5??**

**7.♘b5 d6 8.a3 ♗a5 9.b4 cxb4 10.axb4 ♗xb4 11.♕b2 ♘bc6 12.♕xg7** and White was completely winning after just 12 moves!

The value of knowing and reflecting on such accidents was demonstrated just a couple of days ago at the Olympiad in England's opening match.

**Gawain Jones** (2652)
**Ioannis Damianou** (2153)
Chennai Olympiad 2022 (1)
English Opening

**1.c4 b6 2.♘c3 ♗b7 3.e4 e6 4.♘f3 ♗b4 5.♕c2 c5??**

**6.♘b5 d5 7.e5 ♕e7 8.a3 ♗a5 9.cxd5 exd5**

**10.b4** Same move, disaster on the opposite wing! **10...cxb4 11.♘c7+ ♔d8 12.♘xa8 ♘c6 13.♗b2 ♗xa8 14.♗b5 ♘xe5 15.♘xe5 bxa3 16.♗a6 ♕e6 17.♖c1 b5 18.♕c8+ ♔e7 19.♗xa3+** 1-0.

Another funny example is one where Jeroen Bosch benefited from a trap as Black and then two years later fell

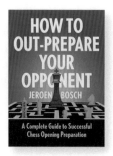

**How to Out-Prepare Your Opponent**
Jeroen Bosch
New In Chess, 2022
★★★★★

into the same trap (slightly disguised) as White! Vigilance always trumps knowledge!

After this warning, the book moves on to consider some other key topics, such as move orders (a big strength of Gawain's *Coffeehouse Repertoire* book that we discussed earlier), novelties (finding, playing and reacting to them), preparing for a specific opponent, and gambits, as well as examining the opening play of Magnus Carlsen (a wonderful example of versatility and cleverness). The book ends with a very nice answer to the (sensible question) of why you shouldn't simply try and play your Black openings with an extra tempo as White!

An excellent book that I would recommend to anyone who wants to improve their effectiveness in the opening phase, without necessarily spending hours stamping concrete variations into their head. I felt that a lot of what I read was insight that I had gained through years of studying the opening and playing professionally, so it's pretty cool to get it for free in a book like this! 5 stars! ∎

## A lot of what I read was insight that I had gained through years of studying, so it's pretty cool to get it for free in a book!

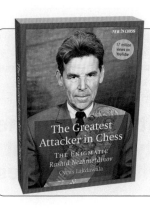

# They are The Champions

The winner of the 2022 Finnish championship is FM Pekka Köykkä. The tournament was a 10-player round-robin played in Helsinki from April 15 to April 23. Pekka, rated number seven at the start, had the tournament of his life and finished clear first with 7 out of 9. With this result, Pekka scored his third IM norm and will be awarded the title soon, as his rating had already passed 2400 in 2018.

During the pandemic, Pekka's chess results and overall mood were down. He even started questioning his chess abilities and wondering whether he would be able to return to his old level. For the Finnish championship, Pekka decided to change his mindset: focus on the moment, enjoy the game, and let go of any expectations based on past results. This meditative state of mind, being fully present, worked miracles. He won his first two games, which boosted his confidence and made him realize that his chess kills were still intact. Pekka accelerated to a score of 5 out of 6 before facing his only tournament loss – against his former trainer IM Mikael Agopov. However, the loss did not shake his confidence, and he convincingly clinched the title with two wins in the last two rounds.

Pekka's training regime consists primarily of opening study and over-the-board practice games with other strong players. Furthermore, he pushes himself to the limit in every rated game he plays, not accepting draws and trying to learn something new from every encounter. Pekka does not find online playing serious enough and prefers to play in-person chess, face to face.

LENNART OOTES

## PEKKA KÖYKKÄ
## Finland

In his daily life, Pekka works on his other passion: film and television. In 2016 and 2017, he produced two comedy shorts as a director and has recently worked as a cameraman and image editor. He likes to make films with humour, since in Pekka's opinion we need a good laugh in these dark days. Pekka is planning to produce another comedy short in 2023 and is currently working on financing the movie.

Pekka's new approach to chess continues to pay him dividends. At the Chess Olympiad in Chennai he had a good start and drew three 2500+ GMs. Pekka eventually finished on the score commensurate with his rating: 5½ out of 10.

In **They are The Champions** we pay tribute to national champions across the globe. For suggestions please write to editors@newinchess.com.

In the following fireworks display from the Rilton Cup in Sweden, Pekka wins with a sequence of only moves.

**Pekka Koykka** (2372)
**Liordis Quesada Vera** (2391)
Stockholm, Rilton Cup, 2019/20

position after 20...g5

**21.♘xa6 gxf4 22.♖ad1! fxg3**
22...♕xa6 loses to 23.♖xd5 ♘df6 24.♖e5. **23.hxg3 ♗d4 24.♘c7!**
Saving the knight as 24...♕xc7 runs into 25.♖xd4. **24...♘e5 25.♖xd4! ♘xf3 26.♖exe4! dxe4** If 26...♘xd4 27.♖g4+ ♔h8 28.♕xc5 winning.

**27.♕c4+!** Forcing the king to give up the protection of ♖f8 and thereby gaining a critical tempo. **27...♔h8 28.♕xc5 ♖c8 29.♖d7 e3 30.♕c3+ ♘e5+ 31.♔h2 ♕e4 32.♖e7 ♖xc7 33.♖e8+ ♔g7 34.♕xc7+** 1-0. ∎

**Jan Timman**

# Stars of the Chennai Olympiad

Youngsters from India and Uzbekistan and a 38-year-old Olympiad 'veteran' from Armenia. **JAN TIMMAN** looks at players that called the tune in Chennai. Did you know that Gukesh's interest in endgames is such that he even composes endgame studies?

**D**ommaraju Gukesh was the absolute hero at the Olympiad in Chennai. Not only his result, but also his way of playing was impressive. I have been following his games with great interest for a good while, especially after he had submitted a study for the study tournament in honour of my 70th birthday. If you are already making a thorough study of endgames at 15 years of age, you are bound to have a great love for the game. Here's the study, with comments from Gukesh himself.

**Gukesh D**
Timman-70 JT 2021

White to play and win

**1.♖a8+ ♔e7 2.♖a7+** 2.♗f6+? ♔f8.
**2...♔d8** 2...♔f8 3.♗g7 mate.
**3.♗f6+ ♘xf6+ 4.exf6 ♗xf6**
**5.♔d6 ♖xe6+** 5...♗e7+ 6.♔c6 ♗b4 7.e7+ ♖xe7 8.♖a8 mate; 5...♗e5+ 6.♔xe5 winning.
**6.♔xe6 ♗c3**
6...♗b2 7.♖a6 g4 8.♖d6+ ♔c7 9.♖c6+ ♔d8 10.♖c2+−.

## If you are already making a thorough study of endgames at 15 years of age, you are bound to have a great love for the game

This position looks like it should be easily winning for White, as the knight is stuck on h4, but because of Black's threat ...g4-g3-g2 or ...g4 and ...♘f3, White has to be extremely precise to win.

**7.♖d7+ ♔c8 8.♖d5!** The concept of this position is trying to combine mating nets against the black king and dominating the black bishop. 8.♖d6? ♗e1! 9.♖c6+ ♔d8 10.♖c4 ♗g3 11.♗b7 ♗c7.
**8...♗b4** 8...♗e1 9.♖c5+ ♔d8 10.♗b7.
**9.♖b5 ♗f8** 9...♗a3 10.♖a5 ♗b4 11.♖a4 ♗e1 12.♖c4+ ♔d8 13.♗b7.
**10.♖b6!**

Now the threat is ♖c6+ ♔d8 ♖c4 and ♗b7, so Black should bring his knight.

**10...g4 11.♔f7!** Aiming to block the d8-square for the black king. 11.♖c6+ ♔d8 12.♖c4 ♘f3 13.♗b7 ♘g5+.

**11...♗a3 12.♔e8**

**12...g3** As the knight is here stuck on the edge of the board, White manages a mating net.

After 12...♘f3, since there is no threat of ...g3-g2 to liquidate, White wins the bishop: 13.♖a6! ♗b4 14.♖c6+ ♔b7 15.♖c4+.

**13.♖c6+ ♔b8 14.♔d7 g2** 14...♔a7 15.♔c8 g2 16.♗d3 g1♕ 17.♖a6 mate.

**15.♖a6 g1♕ 16.♖a8** Mate.

Quite an accomplishment for a 15-year-old! The concept of domination is well thought out and everything is absolutely correct. I would have included his study in the Award, if not for the alternative solutions. On move 7, White can also go 7.♖h7 g4 8.♖xh6, and according to the table base, White will win. And one move later, 8.♔d6 ♗e5+ 9.♔c6 is an alternative way to win.

In Chennai, Gukesh won his first eight games. His eighth win, in the match against the pre-tournament favourites USA, was especially impressive.

**Fabiano Caruana
Gukesh D**
Chennai Olympiad 2022 (8)
Sicilian Defence, Rossolimo Variation

**1.e4 c5 2.♘f3 ♘c6 3.♗b5 g6 4.0-0 ♗g7 5.♗xc6 bxc6 6.♖e1 ♕c7 7.h3 d6 8.e5**

Gukesh raised his score to 8 out of 8 with a win against Fabiano '7 out of 7' Caruana, as India 2 trounced top-seeds USA 3-1.

A new move, although the pawn sacrifice is known in other versions of the Rossolimo Variation. The usual move here is 8.c3, after which White can count on a slight plus.

**8...dxe5 9.d3 c4!** This strategic pawn sacrifice is also known.

**10.♘c3**
White must not capture the pawn, as this would give Black control of the centre after 10.dxc4 f5. This is why White calmly continues his development, trusting that his lead in mobilizing his forces will guarantee sufficient compensation for the pawn.

**10...cxd3 11.cxd3**

**11...♘h6**
Black should certainly not get out of his way to keep the pawn with 11...f6. After 12.d4 exd4 13.♕xd4 e5 14.♕c4 White would already be winning, because Black would be unable to free himself.

What *was* possible was 11...♗e6. I even think it is an important alternative. I don't know anything about Caruana's preparation, of course, but I can imagine the following variation having come up in his study: 12.♕a4 ♖d8 13.♘e4 ♗d5 14.♗d2 ♕b8 15.♖ac1 ♘h6, and now the exchange

sacrifice 16.♖xc6! is very strong. After 16...♗xc6 17.♕xc6+ ♔f8 18.♖c1 White will get a dangerous attack. The text looks good: Black returns the pawn and takes his knight to f5 in order to control the centre. The drawback of the knight manoeuvre is that it's rather time-consuming.
**12.♘xe5 ♘f5 13.♗f4 ♕b7 14.♘a4**

**14...f6** Ambitious, but also risky. The alternative was 14...♗e6, intending to post the bishop on d5. White's best bet then is probably 15.♘c5. After 15...♕xb2 16.♘xe6 fxe6 17.♕c1 he will have reached an endgame that guarantees him a slight plus.
**15.♘f3 0-0 16.d4** This is how White consolidates his position in the centre.
**16...g5** This sharp advance has a concrete drawback, but it was not easy to find a useful alternative.
16...♕d7 would have been strongly met by the energetic 17.g4. After 17...♘xd4 18.♘xd4 e5 the play gets sharp: 19.♕b3+ ♕f7 20.♘xc6 ♗d7 21.♘e7+ ♔h8 22.♗e3 ♗xa4 23.♘xg6+ ♕xg6 24.♕xa4 f5, and Black has some compensation for the pawn.

**17.♗h2** A routine move. Caruana was probably out of his preparation here, otherwise he would certainly have played the intermediate move 17.♘c5!. Over the board, it was not easy to calculate the consequences. Black has two moves:
– 17...♕b6 18.♗d2! ♖f7 (after 18...♘xd4 19.b4! ♘xf3+ 20.♕xf3 e5 21.♖ac1 the bishop pair is powerless, and White controls the position) 19.♕c2 ♖b8 20.♗c3, with a large positional advantage for White. The bishop is excellently placed on c3.
– 17...♕xb2 18.♗c7! is the main point of the knight sortie: taking away the b6-square from the black queen. Although the queen is not in immediate danger, the net has closed, e.g. 18...♖f7 (or 18...♕b4 19.♖c1) 19.♕d3 ♕b5 20.♕c3 ♘d6 21.♘d2, and wins.
**17...h5 18.♖e4 ♕d7 19.♕c2 ♖f7 20.♖ae1 ♗f8**

It's amazing how Gukesh approaches the position. He is building a fortress that will be hard to penetrate, but which does allow for potential counterplay.
**21.♕e2** The computer has a slight preference for 21.a3, but it is certainly not easy to explain the merits of a move like this. It's probably mainly in preparation of the advance b2-b4, but only at precisely the right time.
**21...♕d5** An interesting move was 21...♖g7. Again, Black is threatening to advance his g-pawn, and after 22.♘d2 he could regroup with 22...♕d5 23.♘c3 ♕f7. This concentrates Black's troops on the kingside, which might eventually warrant an attack.
**22.♘c3 ♕d7**

**23.♕c4** Caruana avoids a draw. This is not only understandable, but also supported by the position: White is still slightly better. The problem, however, is that this advantage may very well go up in smoke, after which Black will grab the initiative. White must continue to manoeuvre cautiously. The computer regards the text as not quite accurate. The strongest move was 23.♖d1, which would allow White to execute the advance d4-d5 if he so wished.
**23...♕b7** Gukesh continues to play with his queen for the moment, awaiting White's actions. An alternative was 23...♗b7, intending to complete his development with 24...♖e8 after 24.♘a4.

**24.b4**
Caruana tries to create more room on the queenside, but to no avail.
An interesting alternative was 24.♘a4, trying to penetrate on e6 with the knight. After 24...♕b5 25.♕c2 Black will then have the following possibilities:
– 25...♘g7 26.g4! ♕d5 (26...hxg4 27.hxg4) 27.♘c3 ♕d7 28.♖1e3, and White is exerting pressure on the black position.

– 25...♞h6! (more or less forcing White to make a positional exchange sacrifice) 26.♞c5 ♝f5 27.a4 ♛a5 28.♞e6, and now it is too dangerous to accept the exchange sacrifice. Black will be able to preserve the balance with 28...♜c8!, e.g. 29.♛e2 ♛d5 (accepting the offer will be dangerous for Black after 29...♝xe4 30.♛xe4 ♛f5 31.♛e2!, and Black cannot free himself) 30.♛a6 ♝xe4 31.♛xc8 ♝xf3 32.gxf3 ♞f5 33.♜e4 ♞h4 34.♜xh4! gxh4 35.♚g2, and neither player can make progress.

**24...e6**

Only now, when the white b-pawn has become a target, does Black open de a3-f8 diagonal for his king's bishop. The alternative was 24...a5, after which White will only just be able to preserve the balance with 25.bxa5 ♜xa5 26.a4.

**25.♜b1 ♛d7 26.♜be1 ♛b7 27.♜b1**

**27...♛d7** Gukesh continues to play for repetition, which is a strong tactic, especially from a psychological point of view.

The position allowed for some alternatives, though. Black could have aimed for a queen swap with 27...♛a6, when there could follow: 28.♛xa6 ♝xa6 29.♜xe6 g4 30.hxg4 hxg4 31.♞e1 ♞xd4 32.♜e4 ♜d7 33.♜xg4+ ♚f7, and Black has sufficient compensation for the pawn.

**28.a3**

For the second time, Caruana sidesteps repetition. This time it is a bad decision, since Black will now free himself completely and take matters in his own hands.

**28...a5!**

A strong reaction. Black takes the initiative on the queenside.

**29.♞a4**

Unlike earlier, White could not react with 29.bxa5 ♜xa5 30.a4 here, since

## For the second time, Caruana sidesteps repetition. This time it is a bad decision

this would allow Black to win an exchange with 30...♝a6! 31.♛xe6 ♝d3. In view of this, the text is White's best option to prevent a large deficit.

**29...♛d8!**

Strong play. Now White has no choice but to exchange on a5.

**30.bxa5 ♜xa5**

**31.♞c5?**

An understandable move, but also a serious error that leads to the collapse of the white position. 31.♛c2 was called for, after which Black's best bet was probably 31...♜b5, preventing the

white rook from penetrating via b8.

**31...♛d5**

For the second time, the black queen makes an appearance on d5, this time with decisive force.

**32.♛e2 ♜xa3**

Black has not only won a pawn; he also gets a strong initiative by virtue of having gained space on the queenside.

**33.♜d1 ♜fa7 34.g4**

This move only makes things worse.

**34...hxg4 35.hxg4**

**35...♞h6**

Good enough, but with 35...♜xf3 36.♜xf3 ♞h4 Black could have gone for an elegant win. The point becomes clear after 37.♛b3 ♝xc5 38.♛xd5 cxd5.

**36.♝g3 e5**

This is how the white position gets blown up.

**37.♞xe5 fxe5 38.♜xe5 ♝xg4 39.♛d2 ♛f3 40.♜xg5+ ♜g7 41.♜e1 ♝h3**

Now it's mate in 13!

**42.♝d6 ♝xd6 43.♜xg7+ ♚xg7 44.♛g5+ ♚h7 45.♞e4 ♛xe4**

White resigned.

## Unbeaten Uzbekistan

The Chennai Olympiad was a triumph for youth. The final battle for gold was between the youthful teams of India 2 and Uzbekistan. Some people may find the Uzbeks' overall victory surprising, but they had been my favourites, mainly because Ivan Sokolov was their team captain – and he knows how to guide and motivate young players like no other.

Uzbekistan had 17-year-old Nodirbek Abdusattorov on Board 1. He had already scored some resounding successes, and in Chennai, too, he was on the top of his form. He annotates two of his own games elsewhere in this issue.

The 20-year-old Yakubboev – also called Nodirbek – also did excellently on Board 2. He is a solid player with a very good sense for the initiative. In the match against Germany, he scored the decisive point.

Uzbekistan's Nodirbek Yakubboev (20) had a 2759 performance on Board 2.

**Nodirbek Yakubboev
Matthias Bluebaum**
Chennai Olympiad 2022 (8)

position after 21.g4

If Black continues to play accurately, he will have nothing to fear in this position.
**21...g6?** A serious error. With 21...♗f4! Black could have preserved the balance, e.g. 22.♖cd1 h5 23.♗h4 ♕g6 24.h3 ♖e6, when White can force a draw with 25.♘e7 ♕h6 26.♘f5. There's no more to be got out of it.
**22.♗h4 ♕h8 23.♘d6!**
Bluebaum must have underestimated this. White gets a mighty passed pawn.

**23...♗xd6 24.cxd6 g5 25.♗g3 ♕f6 26.♔g2**
White has a large positional advantage, which Yakubboev systematically converts.
**26...♘b6 27.b3 a5 28.♖c2 ♘d7 29.♖ce2 ♖e6 30.♕d3+ ♔g7 31.♖xe6 fxe6 32.♕e3 ♖e8 33.f4 gxf4 34.♗xf4 ♕g6 35.h3 h5 36.♗e5+ ♔h7 37.g5 ♔g8 38.♗g3 ♔h7 39.h4 ♔g8 40.♕e2 ♔g7 41.♔h2 ♔g8 42.♕d2 ♖a8 43.♖e3 a4 44.b4 b5 45.♕e2 ♖e8 46.♗e5 ♔h7 47.♗f6 ♕f7 48.♗e7 ♕f4+ 49.♔h3 ♔g8 50.♖xe6 ♘f8 51.♖f6 ♕c1 52.♕f3**

Black resigned.

The 16-year-old Javokhir Sindarov was on Board 3 of Uzbekistan. As I have pointed out before, he has an appealingly aggressive style of play. This was also evident in the following game from the important match against Armenia.

**Javokhir Sindarov
Samvel Ter Sahakyan**
Chennai Olympiad 2022 (9)
Sicilian Defence, Najdorf Variation
**1.e4 c5 2.♘f3 d6 3.d4 cxd4 4.♘xd4 ♘f6 5.♘c3 a6 6.♗d3**

A suitable system for those who do not wish to delve into the complicated theory of certain variations of the Najdorf.
**6...e5 7.♘de2 ♗e7 8.0-0 ♗e6 9.f4 exf4 10.♘xf4 ♘c6**

# 16-year-old Javokhir Sindarov has an appealingly aggressive style of play

**11.b3** Shortly before, in Adams-Brkic in Baden-Baden, White had gone for 11.♘xe6. After 11...fxe6 12.♗c4 ♕d7 13.a4 ♖c8 14.♗a2 0-0 15.♗f4 he had a slight advantage. It's a strategically interesting idea to fianchetto the king's bishop. Earlier, 11.♗e3 was also played here.
**11...0-0 12.♗b2 ♘e5 13.♕e1 ♖e8 14.♔h1 ♗f8 15.♖d1 g6 16.h3 ♖c8 17.♕f2 ♗g7 18.♘a4!**

Strong play. White starts with an encirclement strategy.
**18...♕e7 19.♘b6 ♖c6 20.♗d4**
The most ambitious way to play, but one with a tactical drawback. With 20.♗xe5 dxe5 21.♘xe6 ♕xe6 22.♘d5 White could have got some slight superiority.
**20...♕c7 21.♕g1**

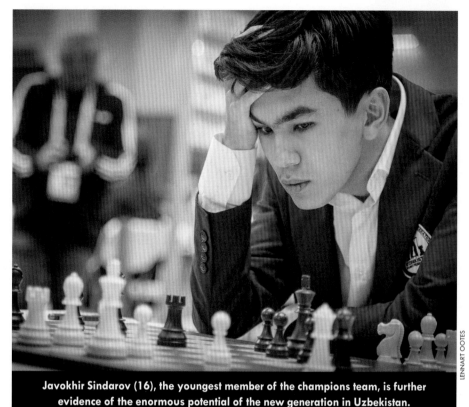

Javokhir Sindarov (16), the youngest member of the champions team, is further evidence of the enormous potential of the new generation in Uzbekistan.

White hides his queen to maintain the pressure.
**21...♕e7**
Black decides to remain passive, allowing the white strategy to become a great success. He should have gone for 21...♘xd3. However, it was difficult to calculate that he would survive the complications after the exit of his strongly centralised knight. The main variation goes as follows: 22.♖xd3 (after 22.cxd3 Black also has 22...♘xe4) 22...♘xe4 23.♘fd5 ♗xd5 24.♘xd5 ♕d8 25.♗xg7 ♔xg7 26.♕d4+,

**ANALYSIS DIAGRAM**

and now 26...♖e5! will just work. White has no way to corner Black any further. After 27.♘f6 ♘xf6 28.♕xe5 dxe5 29.♖xd8 ♖xc2 Black will have no problems.
**22.c4**
This is how White reinforces his central position.
**22...♘fd7**
It was too late for 22...♘xd3. After 23.♖xd3 ♘xe4 24.♗xg7 ♔xg7 25.♕d4+ White will win material.
**23.♘bd5**

The first phase of the encirclement has been completed.

**23...♕h4 24.♗f2** The start of the time-trouble phase: Sindarov hesitates. A strong option was 24.♗b1, preventing the bishop swap. White keeps control of the position.
**24...♕g5 25.♗e3 ♕h4 26.♗f2**
And again 26.♗b1 was called for.
**26...♕h6 27.♗g3**

**27...♕g5** Black misses his chance of counterplay. With 27...g5 28.♘e2 ♘xd3 29.♖xd3 ♘c5 he could have reached equality after, for example, 30.♖e3 ♖cc8 31.♗xd6 ♗xd5 32.♗xc5 ♗xc4 33.bxc4 ♖xc5 34.♖xf7 ♖xc4 35.♖xb7 g4.
**28.♕f2 ♕d8**
The queen is back again. White will now further reinforce his position.
**29.a4 ♖c8 30.♗c2 ♖f8**

**31.♘e3!** Decisive regrouping. The knight is *en route* to f5.
**31...♘c5**
Black should at least have tried 31...b5 in order to get some counterplay. In that case, too, White would have continued with 32.♘f5. After 32... gxf5 33.exf5 ♗xc4 34.bxc4 ♖xc4 35.axb5 axb5 36.♘h5 White would have a decisive advantage.
**32.♘f5!**

The crown on the white strategy. Black is forced to accept the offer.
**32...gxf5 33.exf5 ♗d7 34.♘h5 f6**

**35.b4**
Winning back the piece. 35.♖xd6 would also have been sufficient to win.
**35...♘cd3 36.♗xd3 ♗xa4 37.♖d2 ♗h6 38.♗f4 ♗xf4 39.♘xf4 ♖f7 40.c5 ♘xd3 41.♖xd3 ♗c6 42.♖xd6 ♕f8 43.♘e6**

A mighty square for the knight. Black might as well have resigned here.
**43...♕h6 44.♖fd1 ♖e8 45.♔h2 ♖fe7 46.♖1d4 ♔h8 47.♖h4 ♕c1 48.♕d4 ♖f7 49.♖d8**
Black resigned.

## Armenia's Olympiad star Sargissian

Armenia only lost to Uzbekistan. For the rest, they did exceptionally well. This fits into a tradition – in previous Olympiads they also scored high. This time they had to do it without Levon Aronian, who was playing for the United States, but their team spirit hadn't suffered at all.

A significant part of their success was due to their first-board player Gabriel Sargissian, who usually saves his best form for Olympiads. This time, he started hesitantly with four draws, followed by a defeat against Gukesh. Then he started scoring, in the final phase: which is exactly where it matters in Olympiads. He defeated Caruana, Harikrishna, Mamedyarov and Shirov. In between he drew with Abdusattorov. Sometimes Sargissian had to work hard for the win, e.g. against Harikrishna.

**Gabriel Sargissian**
**Pentala Harikrishna**
Chennai Olympiad 2022 (8)

position after 96.♔b6

For almost 70 moves, Sargissian has held on to a slight endgame advantage. Now the question is how Black should defend himself.
**96...♘b4**
Obvious but insufficient. With 96... a5! Black could have saved himself, giving White two choices:
– 97.♗xc5 ♗xc5+ 98.♔xc5 ♔e5 99.♔b5 ♔d4! 100.c5 (or 100.♔xa5 ♔c5, with a complete blockade) 100...♘c3+ 101.♔c6 ♘d5 102.♔d6 ♘c3 103.c6 ♘b5+ 104.♔d7 ♔c3

JAN TIMMAN

Gabriel Sargissian demonstrated once again that Olympiads bring out the best in him. Replacing Levon Aronian on Board 1, he led Armenia to silver with a 2795 performance.

*LENNART OOTES*

105.♗d1 ♔d2, with a draw.
– 97.♔xa5 ♔f7 98.♗d6 (or 98.♗h6 ♔e7, and White cannot make progress) 98...♔e6 99.♗f4 ♔d7 100.♔b6 ♘b4, and Black has a fortress.
**97.♗b1 a5** Too late. **98.♗xc5 ♗xc5+ 99.♔xc5**

**99...♔d7** After 99...♔e5 100.♗h7 Black would be in zugzwang.
**100.♔b6 ♔c8 101.♔xa5 ♘c6+ 102.♔b6** Black resigned.

In other games, victory was offered on a plate. Mamedyarov made a mistake as White in the opening phase and was already lost after 16 moves. In the final round, against Shirov, things also proceeded smoothly.

**Gabriel Sargissian**
**Alexey Shirov**
Chennai Olympiad 2022 (11)

position after 14...0-0-0

The opening has not gone entirely according to plan for Black.
**15.♕d2!** A strong move. White is threatening 16.♗g5, while also planning a queen sortie to a5.
**15...g6?** A lapse in concentration. Shirov makes a terrible mistake here. After 15...♗e7 16.♕a5 ♔b8 17.♔b1

## Gabriel Sargissian usually saves his best form for Olympiads

White would have had an advantage, but the situation is not yet alarming for Black.
**16.♗g5 ♕h5**

**17.♗e2** After 17.♗xd8 ♗h6 Black gets his way. The text-move is the most convincing refutation of Black's 15th move, but 17.f4 was also winning, for example 17...♗h6 18.♗e2 ♕h3 19.♗f6! e5 20.♔b1 ♗xf4 21.♕b4 exd4 22.♗xh8 ♖xh8 23.♕xd4.
**17...♗b4 18.♕e3**

Now White is threatening 19.f4, winning the queen. Black must give an exchange without a scintilla of compensation.
**18...e5 19.♗xd8 ♖xd8 20.dxe5 ♕xe5 21.♖xd8+ ♔xd8 22.♖d1+ ♔e7 23.f4 ♕c5+ 24.♔b1 ♕xe3 25.fxe3 ♘e8 26.e5 ♗c5 27.♗g4 f5 28.exf6+ ♘xf6 29.♗f3 h6 30.h4 ♔e6 31.♔c2 h5 32.♔d3 ♗e7 33.♖g1 ♔f7 34.♔e2 ♘d7 35.♗e4 ♘f8 36.♖h1 ♘d7 37.♗c2 ♗f6 38.e4 ♗d4 39.e5 ♘f8 40.♔d3 c5 41.♔e4 b6 42.b4 ♔e7 43.♗b3 ♗f2 44.b5 ♘d7 45.♗c4 ♘f8 46.♖h3 ♗e1 47.f5 gxf5+ 48.♔xf5 ♘d7 49.♖a3**
Black resigned. ∎

# Anna Cramling

**CURRENT ELO:** 2065

**DATE OF BIRTH:** April 30, 2002

**PLACE OF BIRTH:** Malaga, Spain

**PLACE OF RESIDENCE:** Stockholm, Sweden

**What is your favourite city?**
There are many, but I love Amsterdam and would love to live there someday.

**What was the last great meal you had?**
I always get *really* hungry after streaming, so a pasta carbonara I had the other day after streaming.

**What drink brings a smile to your face?**
A cold lemonade!

**Which book would you give to a friend?**
Maybe a chess book, to see if they get inspired to pick up chess.

**What book are you currently reading?**
The last book I read was *One Flew over The Cuckoo's Nest* in high school.

**What is your all-time favourite movie?**
I don't really have a favourite movie, but I liked *The Wolf of Wall Street*.

**And your favourite TV series?**
Probably *Outlander*.

**Do you have a favourite actor?**
Leonardo Di Caprio.

**And a favourite actress?**
Julia Roberts.

**What music do you listen to?**
Lots of Lana Del Rey and Billie Eilish.

**Is there a painting that moves you?**
*The Starry Night* by Vincent van Gogh.

**What is your earliest chess memory?**
Seeing my parents play in chess tournaments. I clearly remember walking around the Olympiad in 2008 and wishing I could play!

**Who is your favourite chess player?**
Probably Garry Kasparov, because of his amazing attacking style.

**Is there a chess book that had a profound influence on you?**
Jacob Aagaard's *Grandmaster Preparation* series.

**What was your best result ever?**
Beating a 2498 IM in an Open in Spain.

**And the best game you played?**
My win against Govhar Beydullayeva, then rated 2307, at the European U-18 Championship in 2019.

**What is your favourite square?**
The d4-square.

**What are chess players particularly good at (except for chess)?**
Remembering *a lot* of really random stuff.

**Facebook, Instagram, Snapchat, or?**
Instagram 100%.

**Who do you follow on Twitter?**
Way too many.

**What is your life motto?**
There's no better time than now.

**When were you happiest?**
Probably right now!

**Who or what would you like to be if you weren't yourself?**
I'd love to be an actress or TV host. I am 100% sure I'd work with content creation somehow, even if I didn't play chess.

**Which three people would you like to invite for dinner?**
Paul Morphy, Bobby Fischer and Garry Kasparov. That would be interesting!

**What is the best piece of advice you were ever given?**
'When you see a good move, look for a better one.' – Emanuel Lasker.

**Is there something you'd love to learn?**
How to sing. I've always been terrible at it.

**What would people be surprised to know about you?**
I studied Mandarin for two years when I was very young! I have forgotten almost everything, though.

**Where is your favourite place in the world?**
On a plane. I *love* travelling.

**What is your greatest fear?**
Doing work I don't love.

**And your greatest regret?**
Not taking chess seriously sooner.

**If you could change one thing in the chess world, what would it be?**
Chess should become mainstream and be accessible to everyone.

**Is a knowledge of chess useful in everyday life?**
Chess has helped me in many ways, but especially with concentration and patience, which are important skills in life.

**What is the best thing that was ever said about chess?**
'I have come to the personal conclusion that while all artists are not chess players, all chess players are artists.' – Marcel Duchamp.